DATE DUE

			PRINTED IN U.S.A.

Symbolism

GREAT ARTISTS OF THE WESTERN WORLD

Symbolism

Dante Gabriel Rossetti

——❦——

Odilon Redon

——❦——

Gustav Klimt

——❦——

Edvard Munch

MARSHALL CAVENDISH · LONDON · NEW YORK · SYDNEY

Staff Credits

Editors	Clive Gregory LLB Sue Lyon BA (Honours)	**Picture Researchers**	Vanessa Fletcher BA (Honours) Flavia Howard BA (Honours) Jessica Johnson BA
Art Editors	Chris Legee BFA Kate Sprawson BA (Honours) Keith Vollans LSIAD		
		Production Controllers	Tom Helsby Alan Stewart BSc
Deputy Editor	John Kirkwood BSc (Honours)		
		Secretary	Lynn Smail
Sub-editors	Caroline Bugler BA (Honours), MA Sue Churchill BA (Honours) Alison Cole BA, MPhil Jenny Mohammadi Nigel Rodgers BA (Honours), MA Penny Smith Will Steeds BA (Honours), MA	**Editorial Director**	Maggi McCormick
		Publishing Manager	Robert Paulley BSc
		Managing Editor	Alan Ross BA (Honours)
Designers	Stuart John Julie Stanniland	**Consultant and Authenticator**	Sharon Fermor BA (Honours) Lecturer in the Extra-Mural Department of London University and Lecturer in Art History at Sussex University

Reference Edition Published 1988

Published by Marshall Cavendish Corporation
147 West Merrick Road
Freeport, Long Island
N.Y. 11520

Typeset by Litho Link Ltd., Welshpool
Printed and Bound by Dai Nippon
Printing Co., Hong Kong Ltd.

Library of Congress Cataloging-in-Publication Data

Main entry under title:

Great Artists of the Western World II.

Includes index.
1. Artists – Biography. I. Marshall Cavendish Corporation.
N40.G774 1988   709'.2'2 [B]   88–4317
ISBN 0–86307–900–8 (set)

ISBN 0–86307–900–8 (set)
       0–86307–762–5 (vol)

Preface

Looking at pictures can be one of the greatest pleasures that life has to offer. Note, however, those two words 'can be'; all too many of us remember all too clearly those grim afternoons of childhood when we were dragged, bored to tears and complaining bitterly, through room after room of Italian primitives by well-meaning relations or tight-lipped teachers. It was enough to put one off pictures for life – which, for some of us, was exactly what it did.

For if gallery-going is to be the fun it should be, certain conditions must be fulfilled. First, the pictures we are to see must be good pictures. Not necessarily **great** pictures – even a few of these can be daunting, while too many at a time may prove dangerously indigestible. But they must be well-painted, by good artists who know precisely both the effect they want to achieve and how best to achieve it. Second, we must limit ourselves as to quantity. Three rooms – four at the most – of the average gallery are more than enough for one day, and for best results we should always leave while we are still fresh, well before satiety sets in. Now I am well aware that this is a counsel of perfection: sometimes, in the case of a visiting exhibition or, perhaps, when we are in a foreign city with only a day to spare, we shall have no choice but to grit our teeth and stagger on to the end. But we shall not enjoy ourselves quite so much, nor will the pictures remain so long or so clearly in our memory.

The third condition is all-important: we must know something about the painters whose work we are looking at. And this is where this magnificent series of volumes – one of which you now hold in your hands – can make all the difference. No painting is an island: it must, if it is to be worth a moment's attention, express something of the personality of its painter. And that painter, however individual a genius, cannot but reflect the country, style and period, together with the views and attitudes of the people among whom he or she was born and bred. Even a superficial understanding of these things will illuminate a painting for us far better than any number of spotlights, and if in addition we have learnt something about the artist as a person – life and loves, character and beliefs, friends and patrons, and the places to which he or she travelled – the interest and pleasure that the work will give us will be multiplied a hundredfold.

Great Artists of the Western World will provide you with just such an insight into the life and work of some of the outstanding painters of Europe and America. The text is informative without ever becoming dry or academic, not limiting itself to the usual potted biographies but forever branching out into the contemporary world outside and beyond workshop or studio. The illustrations, in colour throughout, have been dispensed in almost reckless profusion. For those who, like me, revel in playing the Attribution Game – the object of which is to guess the painter of each picture before allowing one's eye to drop to the label – the little sections on 'Trademarks' are a particularly happy feature; but every aficionado will have particular preferences, and I doubt whether there is an art historian alive, however distinguished, who would not find some fascinating nugget of previously unknown information among the pages that follow.

This series, however, is not intended for art historians. It is designed for ordinary people like you and me – and for our older children – who are fully aware that the art galleries of the world constitute a virtually bottomless mine of potential enjoyment, and who are determined to extract as much benefit and advantage from it as they possibly can. All the volumes in this collection will enable us to do just that, expanding our knowledge not only of art itself but also of history, religion, mythology, philosophy, fashion, interior decoration, social customs and a thousand other subjects as well. So let us not simply leave them around, flipping idly through a few of their pages once in a while. Let us read them as they deserve to be read – and welcome a new dimension in our lives.

John Julius Norwich is a writer and broadcaster who has written histories of Venice and of Norman Sicily as well as several works on history, art and architecture. He has also made over twenty documentary films for television, including the recent Treasure Houses of Britain series which was widely acclaimed after repeated showings in the United States.

Lord Norwich is Chairman of the Venice in Peril Fund, and member of the Executive Committee of the British National Trust, an independently funded body established for the protection of places of historic interest and natural beauty.

John Julius Norwich

Contents

Introduction

The Symbolist movement became a dominant force in European painting in the last decades of the 19th century. Its development varied from country to country, but its prevailing aim, shared by all its adherents, was to counter the spread of naturalism and realism and to reintroduce a dimension of spirituality into the realms of art.

Rossetti and the PRB

In England, the movement grew out of Romanticism and found its first flowerings in the work of the Pre-Raphaelite Brotherhood (PRB). The members of the latter group drew heavily on certain

The artists
(from the top) Rossetti in 1853 in a portrait by William Holman Hunt; a self-portrait of Munch, aged 32; Redon in his late twenties in a self-portrait; Klimt photographed in 1908.

Tate Gallery, London

Romantic features – most notably in their taste for medievalism and the exotic, and in their reliance on literary themes – but replaced its emotional vigour with a suggestive and poetic air that was to be much admired by the Symbolists.

To the literal-minded Victorians, however, it was precisely these evocative qualities that proved so baffling. One of the most viciously attacked Pre-Raphaelite paintings, for example, was Millais' Sir Isumbras at the Ford, which the critics ridiculed for its apparent lack of meaning. At this time, Rossetti was concentrating on private commissions for watercolours and so escaped this sort of censure, even though his works of the period were very similar in tone. Pictures like The Blue Closet (p.18) and The Tune of Seven Towers (p.29) had all the ingredients of narrative painting, but their subject-matter remained defiantly obscure.

Instead of a specific story-line, the Pre-Raphaelites were attempting to create mood pictures. Sir Isumbras, significantly, was subtitled A Dream of the Past by the artist, while Rossetti's Wedding of St George . . . (p.28) was described by a contemporary as 'like a golden dim dream . . . a sense of secret enclosure in palace chambers far apart . . .'. Rossetti had contributed to this mysterious effect by enclosing his figures in a cramped and unreal environment, and by using a series of conflicting patterns to confuse the spectator's eye. These techniques were later to be pushed to extreme limits by Klimt.

Rossetti maintained his ambiguous approach to subject-matter after his return to oil painting. The sensuous studies of women, which were his principal achievements during the 1860s and 1870s, had only the most nominal of themes. In some cases, such as Monna Vanna (p.31), the title was chosen after the picture was completed – Rossetti originally called it 'Venus Veneta' – while in others (for example, The Blue Blower, p.15), the vagueness of the title confirmed that the artist's true interest lay in poetic colour harmonies.

Rossetti's exercises in colour and form were echoed in the paintings of Aesthetic artists, such as Albert Moore and Whistler. The latter even went so

The symbolism of the rose
Traditionally, roses symbolize youth and beauty, and it is particularly fitting that they dominate Rossetti's The Beloved, since the work was inspired by the description of the bride (or beloved) of The Song of Solomon.

far as to adopt abstract titles, such as 'Harmonies' and 'Arrangements', for many of his compositions. Subsequently, the main elements of Aestheticism and Pre-Raphaelitism were united in the work of Burne-Jones and it was through him that English art made its greatest impact on the mainstream of Symbolist developments in France.

The Literary Influence
There, the earliest impulses of Symbolist painting can be traced back to the 1860s, when they were spearheaded by Moreau and Puvis de Chavannes. Both these artists were affiliated to the Academic tradition and continued to provide an alternative form of idealistic painting during the period when naturalism – under the auspices of Realism and Impressionism – held sway. In the 1880s, as the latter began to lose impetus, these undercurrents surfaced as a fully fledged movement.

The strength of Symbolist painting in France was largely due to the literary trends that had preceded it. This had a twofold advantage. Symbolist writers provided a firm, theoretical basis for the movement – something that had been patently lacking in England – and they also bequeathed to artists a rich stock of imagery that was ultimately to spread throughout Europe.

The Symbolist ethic had many ramifications but its central thesis was contained in Baudelaire's notion of 'correspondences'. Through this Neo-Platonic concept, it was held that natural forms were nothing more than the living symbols of a higher reality and that the artist's imagination was the key that could reveal these spiritual truths.

This literary strain of Symbolism was very much to the fore in Redon's art. His greatest contributions to the movement were effected in his uncoloured lithographs and charcoal drawings and, in these, he made no secret of his sources. During the 1880s, there were major lithographic series devoted to such Symbolist luminaries as Poe, Baudelaire and Flaubert. However, Redon's lithographs were not simple illustrations to these authors. Rather, they were designed to evoke the spirit of their work.

Redon's distinctive imagery combined the microscopic organisms, which he had learnt about from Clavaud (see p.46), with a range of haunting motifs that derived from Moreau. In particular, he made frequent use of the latter's favourite image: the severed head. This featured in both the episode of Salome with John the Baptist and the

Portraits, opposite from the top: Birmingham City Museums and Art Gallery; National Gallery, Oslo; Réunion des Musées Nationaux/Musée d'Orsay; Bildarchiv der Osterreiche Nationalbibliothek, Vienna

dismemberment of Orpheus (p.54), probably the most fertile themes in the Symbolist repertoire. The immense popularity of these two subjects can be ascribed to their emphasis on male vulnerability at the hands of the femme fatale (both Orpheus and St John met their deaths at the hands of vicious women). In addition, in a variant of the Orpheus myth, the victim's severed head was shown, still singing, as it floated on the waters, and this macabre image of the immortality of the arts appealed greatly to Symbolist sensibilities.

Predatory Women

Both Moreau and Redon earned high praise in Huysmans A Rebours (see p.68) and it was in this novel that the final strands of the Symbolist movement fell into place. Alongside the Aesthetic insistence on a moral beauty, Huysmans advocated a code of Decadence, epitomized by his worship of artificiality and unnatural pleasures.

The imagery in this and similar works gained very wide currency for a brief time but, by the end of the century, they were largely played out and, when Redon employed sphinxes and severed heads in his later pastels (p.66), they constituted little more than decorative devices. With Munch, however, Symbolist imagery retained its potency for much longer, as it struck a deep chord within his own troubled personality.

Munch was well aware that his neurosis and, in particular, his fear of women was the mainspring of his art and, until his breakdown, he allowed this to inspire some of the most unsettling pictures in the entire Symbolist canon. His Madonnas were tainted with sex and death, while the vampirism of his Kiss was one of the most compelling images of the femme fatale and prompted numerous imitations. Even where the subject was innocence, as in Puberty (p.121), Munch introduced menacing shadows to cast a cloud over the scene.

The artist's intention was to exhibit his works together as a 'Frieze of Life', when he hoped they would create a 'symphonic effect'. This musical analogy was a feature of the period, as Symbolist artists were at pains to show the similarities between music and painting. Accordingly, musical themes figured prominently in the work of Rossetti (pp.15, 18, 29, 32) and Klimt (pp.88, 93), and it is significant that Orpheus was selected as the universal representative of the arts.

The attempt to engender a 'musical' style of painting highlighted the second main category of Symbolism. For, rather than rely purely on literary motifs, many artists chose to use simplified forms and colours to underline their anti-naturalistic aims. Both these traits were combined in Munch's work, but in a uniquely disturbing synthesis. His use of sinuous distortions to evoke emotions rather than ideas meant that, while his artistic vocabulary might be Symbolist, his message was closer to that of Expressionism.

Other manifestations of this stylized form of Symbolism placed a much greater emphasis on ornamentation. In France, Gauguin and the Nabis led the way in promoting a decorative manner that culminated in Art Nouveau. In Germanic countries, the equivalent trend was known as Jugendstil and this movement reached the peak of its refinement in the work of Gustav Klimt.

Stylized Forms

Klimt's pictures still retained the well-worn imagery of the Decadents, including predatory femmes fatales (p.86), suffocating embraces (pp.84-5, 99) and severed heads – though the latter were now suggested with greater subtlety, through suitable neck-wear (pp.90, 94) or swathes of hair (pp.95 and 96). However, Klimt breathed new life into these conventions by clothing his erotic visions in an almost oppressive richness of surface ornament that would, doubtless, have proved a delight to Huysmans.

The tone of Klimt's paintings was marked by a sexual frankness that probably derived from the theories of Freud – then the subject of much discussion in Vienna – and which certainly caused his fall from grace with the authorities. In pursuing his ends, the artist reinforced his literary themes with a wealth of semi-abstract stylization and this combination is reminiscent of Munch's approach, even though Klimt's target was clearly the libido rather than the psyche.

The environment in which Klimt's style blossomed was swept away by World War I and, in this context, it may appear like the last flourish of a dying civilization. However, Symbolism opened more doors than it closed. The literary aspects of its development provided a direct link with Surrealism, while the stylized, 'musical' implications of the movement inspired abstract artists such as Kandinsky and Mondrian and, ultimately, laid the foundations of modern art.

William Holman Hunt: Rossetti in 1853/Birmingham City Museums and Art Gallery

DANTE GABRIEL ROSSETTI

1828-1882

The son of an Italian writer and political refugee, Dante Gabriel Rossetti was brilliantly gifted as a poet as well as a painter. He was a dominant and charismatic personality, and at the age of 20 was the driving force behind the Pre-Raphaelite Brotherhood, the secret society that aimed to reform British art. Despising convention, Rossetti shunned the official art world, preferring to sell his paintings to private collectors.

Rossetti's favourite subject was beautiful women – for the last 20 years of his life he painted little else. Handsome, charming and successful, he was an intensely attractive man, but his love-life was strained. His wife died within two years of their marriage, and he then idolized the wife of his friend William Morris. In his last years he became an eccentric recluse fighting drugs and alcohol, and died paralyzed at the age of 53.

The Passionate Victorian

The son of an exiled Italian, Rossetti never submitted to social conventions. After shocking the artistic establishment, he lived apparently 'in sin', and died an eccentric recluse.

Key Dates

1828 born in London

1845 enrols at Royal Academy Schools

1848 Pre-Raphaelite Brotherhood founded

1854 meets art critic John Ruskin

1856 becomes friendly with William Morris and Edward Burne-Jones

1857 meets Jane Morris

1860 marries Lizzie Siddal

1862 Lizzie dies. Moves to Tudor House, Chelsea

1870 completes *Beata Beatrix*, a memorial to his dead wife

1877 paints *Astarte Syriaca*

1881 suffers a stroke

1882 dies in Birchington-on-Sea

National Portrait Gallery, London

The artist at 19
This self-portrait shows Rossetti in 1847, the year before he established the Pre-Raphaelite Brotherhood. With his long hair, brooding eyes and passionate manner, Rossetti was a striking figure, even as a young man.

Rossetti's London
(below) Although Rossetti was three-quarters Italian, he never visited his parents' homeland. Apart from minor trips abroad, and periods spent at Kelmscott Manor in Oxfordshire, he lived virtually all of his life in London.

Dante Gabriel Rossetti was born in London on 12 May 1828, and grew up in one of the most remarkable families in Victorian England. His father, Gabriele Pasquale Giuseppe Rossetti, was an Italian poet and scholar who had fled his native country after being sentenced to death for his involvement in a revolutionary secret society. Gabriele settled in England in 1824 and two years later married Frances Mary Lavinia Polidori, a one-time governess and teacher who was the daughter of another Italian exile and an English mother.

Dante Gabriel was the second of four children, all born within four years of each other, and all intellectually gifted. They were brought up to speak Italian as well as English, and Maria, the eldest, became a scholarly authority on the Italian language. Christina won fame as one of the finest poets of her period, while William Michael established himself as one of the leading art critics of the day. Yet their mother later made the illuminating comment that it might have been better to have 'a little less intellect in the family so as to allow for a little more common sense'.

Bridgeman Art Library

Gabriele earned his living by teaching Italian, and in 1831 became Professor of Italian at King's College in London. In spite of its impressive title, the post was not well paid, and the family home in Charlotte Street (now Hallam Street) near Regent's Park was fairly humble. However, the job meant that he could have his sons taught free or at reduced fees at King's College School. So Dante Gabriel and William Michael both had a good education, which included drawing lessons.

AN INDOLENT PUPIL

Dante Gabriel's childhood love of drawing was so intense that his brother later observed that it was always understood that he would become a painter. When he left King's College School at the age of 14, Dante Gabriel was sent to Sass's Art School, a drawing academy that was the normal stepping stone to the Royal Academy Schools, to which he progressed in 1845. His three-year period at Sass's was longer than usual, because he hated having to submit to the academic discipline of drawing from antique sculpture, and was an indolent pupil: 'As soon as a thing is imposed on me as an obligation, my aptitude for doing it is gone; what I *ought* to do is what I *can't* do.'

The young student Rossetti was a striking

Mary Evans Picture Library

An Italian father
(below) Gabriele Rossetti, poet, scholar and political refugee, arrived in England, via Malta, in 1824. His son – named after Dante Alighieri, the great Italian poet – inherited Gabriele's love of literature, and became a poet as well as a painter.

Rebel at the Academy
(above) Rossetti studied at the Royal Academy, but rejected both its academic teaching and the 'lifeless' paintings that hung there. Instead of exhibiting at the RA, he preferred to show his paintings at the Free Exhibition sited near Hyde Park.

figure. He was remarkably handsome, with beautiful blue-grey eyes and flowing locks of auburn hair, and he already possessed a personal magnetism that made him the centre of attraction in any company. As his brother recalled, 'Apart from his mental gifts, the quality most innate in him appears to have been dominance. He was imperative, vehement, at times angrily passionate; but his anger was a sudden and passing impulse, and to sulk or bear a grudge was not in him at all.'

LETTER TO A PAINTER

But Rossetti was no happier with the routine at the Royal Academy than he had been with that at Sass's and in March 1848 he wrote to a painter he admired, Ford Madox Brown (then aged 26), asking him to take him on as his pupil. The letter was so gushingly effusive that Brown, who had a prickly temperament, thought that it was intended sarcastically and stormed round to the Rossetti house with a cudgel. Rossetti soon convinced him of his sincerity and Brown agreed to accept him as an informal pupil, while he was still officially attached to the Royal Academy.

Although Rossetti was impressed by the seriousness and literary inspiration of Brown's paintings, he was dismayed when Brown tried to teach him the same traditional, academic skills that he had already rejected. He soon abandoned the idea of an apprenticeship with Brown, but they remained lifelong friends.

As he approached his twentieth birthday, Rossetti was still uncertain whether he should make literature or painting his career. He sent

The Lovely Lizzie

Rossetti met his future wife Elizabeth Siddal in about 1850. 'A most beautiful creature – tall, finely framed, with a lofty neck . . . and a lavish heavy wealth of coppery-golden hair', she had been introduced to him by the painter Walter Deverell, who had spotted her in a milliner's shop. Her soulful good-looks made her the perfect model for the Pre-Raphaelites, but she also became a painter and poet in her own right. She died of an overdose of laudanum in 1862, not quite two years after marrying Rossetti.

A melancholy beauty
Rossetti made this tender drawing of his 'Ideal Beloved' Lizzie in 1855, five years before their eventual marriage.

Model for Shakespeare
(right) Lizzie Siddal's delicate features appear in many Pre-Raphaelite paintings. This detail of Holman Hunt's illustration from Two Gentlemen of Verona, *shows her as Sylvia.*

'Valentine Rescuing Sylvia' (detail)/Birmingham City Museums and Art Gallery

The Mansell Collection

some of his poems to Leigh Hunt, a distinguished poet and critic, who praised them warmly, but sensibly pointed out that it was much harder to make a living as a poet than as a painter: 'If you paint as well as you write', advised Hunt, 'you may be a rich man.' Although he was overflowing with ideas, Rossetti had not yet produced any significant work as a painter, but the way forward opened up to him as his friendship grew with two fellow-students at the Royal Academy: William Holman Hunt and John Everett Millais.

THE PRE-RAPHAELITE BROTHERHOOD

These three young men were widely different in temperament and talents, but they shared a sense of dismay at what they considered the moribund state of British art. In order to express their rejection of the lifeless artistic conventions which they saw as stemming from the 16th century master Raphael, Rossetti, Millais and Hunt decided to call themselves 'Pre-Raphaelites'. They were joined by Rossetti's brother and three other friends, and in 1848 the seven young men formed a secret society which they called the Pre-Raphaelite Brotherhood.

Rossetti's first major oil painting, *The Girlhood of Mary Virgin* (p.24), ·was the first painting exhibited bearing the Brotherhood's initials PRB. It was warmly praised, and was bought by the

Ruskin and Rossetti
In 1854, the art critic John Ruskin wrote to Rossetti, expressing admiration for his work. It was the start of a stormy but long-lasting friendship, in which Ruskin adopted the roles of both champion and mentor.

BBC Hulton Picture Library

Tudor House
After Lizzie's tragic death, Rossetti moved from Blackfriars to the grand 'Tudor House' in Cheyne Walk, Chelsea. For a short while, he shared his home with the novelist George Meredith and the poet Algernon Swinburne, until the latter's childish, and often drunken, behaviour proved too much to bear.

Fanny Cornforth
Rossetti's The Blue Bower *features his mistress and model Fanny Cornforth. While Lizzie Siddal was his ideal love, Rossetti enjoyed a more physical relationship with Fanny – a forthright cockney woman, some four years his senior.*

probably seemed that they 'lived in sin' for several years before their eventual marriage in 1860. But their relationship was unusual by any standards, and often strained. Though Rossetti became more and more obsessed with Lizzie, he saw her as an 'ideal beloved' – who should be worshipped, but not touched. Like many Victorian men, Rossetti divided women into two classes – angels and whores – and sexual intimacy with Lizzie would have sent her tumbling from the pedestal on which he had placed her.

A MISTRESS FOR LIFE

So he looked elsewhere to relieve his sexual tensions. His most long-lasting affair was with a woman called Sarah Cox (later known as Fanny Cornforth), whom he first met in about 1858. According to one account, he picked her up in the Strand, where she had attracted his attention in a none-too-subtle fashion by cracking nuts between her teeth and throwing the shells at him. Buxom, healthy and with an earthy sense of humour, she was the complete opposite of the fragile Lizzie. And though the relationship broke up after Lizzie and Rossetti's marriage, it was later resumed and continued almost until his death.

Dowager Marchioness of Bath for 80 guineas. Rossetti's career as a painter seemed to be taking off, but in the following year he was brought sharply down to earth. When the meaning of the initials PRB leaked out, he and his associates were savagely attacked in the press, and denounced as upstarts who had besmirched the name of Raphael – who was almost universally regarded as the greatest painter who had ever lived.

Rossetti was so upset by the criticism that he vowed never again to exhibit in public. He rarely broke the vow, and in the decade 1850-60 he virtually abandoned oils and worked on small water-colours. The Pre-Raphaelite Brotherhood was breaking up and Rossetti, who had for a time shared a studio with Hunt, found rooms of his own at 14 Chatham Place, near Blackfriars Bridge. Although he was not exhibiting, his water-colours began to sell well, often to contacts of the famous art critic John Ruskin, whom he met in 1854.

Ruskin was one of several new friends who had a great impact on Rossetti's life in the 1850s. In 1850 (or perhaps late 1849) he met his future wife Elizabeth Siddal, the first of the beautiful women ('stunners', as he called them) who were to haunt his imagination and provide him with unending inspiration for his painting. The red-haired Lizzie was 'discovered' by Walter Deverell, a painter friend of Rossetti, when she was working in a milliner's shop in Leicester Square.

Lizzie may well have been in love with the handsome and charming Deverell, who died aged 26 in 1854. But although she became very sickly after his death, a deep mutual attraction gradually grew between her and Rossetti.

From an outside observer's viewpoint, it

A Teacher and Friend

Having studied art throughout Europe, Ford Madox Brown was struggling to establish himself as a painter of early historical subjects when Rossetti wrote to him fervently requesting painting lessons. Their pupil-teacher relationship only lasted a few weeks, but they remained affectionate friends. Though Brown was sympathetic to the aims of the Pre-Raphaelite Brotherhood, he never joined it. In 1861, however, he joined Rossetti as a founder member of William Morris's decorating company.

BBC Hulton Picture Library

Ford Madox Brown
Only seven years older than Rossetti, Brown was already a widower when they met in 1848, and renowned for his 'peppery' temperament. However, he generously agreed to give his young admirer free tuition.

The Last of England
This picture was inspired by the emigration of the Pre-Raphaelite artist Thomas Woolner. The fluttering ribbons took Brown four weeks to paint.

Birmingham City Museums and Art Gallery

In 1856, Rossetti formed a friendship with two undergraduates at Oxford, William Morris and Edward Burne-Jones. The following year he helped them and several other young artists to decorate the debating chamber of the Oxford Union with scenes from Arthurian legend. And in the 1860s Rossetti and Burne-Jones were two of the leading artists to work for Morris's new firm of 'fine art workmen'.

In May 1861, 12 months after their marriage, Lizzie gave birth to a still-born daughter. By the following spring she, too, was dead: her constant ill health and depressions led her to rely on laudanum, an addictive medicine containing opium, and she died of an overdose. Rossetti was devastated. Indeed, he was so grief-stricken that he had the only complete manuscript of his poems buried with her. (He had them exhumed in 1869 and published in 1870.)

THE MOVE TO CHELSEA

In October 1862, the widowed Rossetti moved from Blackfriars to the grand Tudor House in Chelsea's Cheyne Walk, where Fanny Cornforth reappeared in his life, as his model, mistress and housekeeper. His paintings of her were more richly sensuous than those of the ethereal Lizzie, and they sold well. Rossetti was a hard businessman in his relationships with picture dealers, and in the 1860s his income rose to £3,000 per year.

When Rossetti discovered another voluptuous model, Alexa Wilding, in the street, he could easily afford to pay her an annual retainer. She sat for many of his most splendid paintings, but the face that more than any other dominates Rossetti's later work is that of William Morris' wife, Jane. Rossetti had met Janey in 1857, two years before she married Morris. Like Lizzie, she was tall and stunningly attractive, and like Lizzie she became a permanent semi-invalid. Fanny Cornforth (and others) might satisfy Rossetti's physical needs, but Janey fulfilled his desire for an ideal, mystical love.

In 1872, Rossetti (now wealthy enough to employ assistants) suffered a physical collapse. He was drinking heavily and also taking the

Janey and the wombat
William Morris's beautiful, dark-haired wife became the object of Rossetti's adoration after Lizzie's death. In this drawing of Janey, the artist shows her with the pet wombat from his garden menagerie.

Fotomas Index

anaesthetic drug chloral in an attempt to stave off chronic insomnia. Although he recovered, most of the last 10 years of his life was spent as a virtual recluse in Chelsea. Alcohol and drugs took a heavy toll, and often his hands shook so much that he was unable to work.

Rossetti had changed greatly in appearance since his days as a beautiful youth. He became stout, and his darkly-ringed eyes gave him a rather saturnine look. But he could still be a compelling figure and a brilliant conversationalist. He also gained a reputation as an eccentric. His house was full of antiques and all manner of bric-à-brac and in the garden he kept a menagerie of exotic animals including armadillos, racoons, and peacocks. Most of the animals were bought to satisfy passing whims and they were often neglected, but he had a touching affection for a pet wombat and wrote a poem lamenting its death.

The Rossetti family
The author Lewis Carroll took this photograph of the Rossetti family in the Tudor House garden in 1863. The artist and his brother William Michael stand on either side of their sister Christina, and their mother. The artist's father had died nine years before.

A Victorian Interior
(left) This water-colour, painted the year of Rossetti's death, shows him at home with his friend and legal adviser Theodore Watts-Dunton, amid the collection of antiques and bric-à-brac in the Tudor House. It was painted by Rossetti's assistant, H.T. Dunn.

Ill, depressed, and old before his time, Rossetti rarely left the house in his final years, except to visit his old friend Madox Brown or his mother and his sister Christina. And in December 1881, the ailing artist had a stroke that left him partially paralyzed in the left arm and leg. He ended his long relationship with Fanny – the cockney 'Helephant' whom his friends had never accepted – and in February 1882 went to convalesce at Birchington-on-Sea, near Margate in Kent.

Rossetti died there aged 53, on 9 April – Easter Sunday. He had left instructions that he was not to be buried beside Lizzie in Highgate Cemetery (perhaps because of feelings of guilt at having desecrated her grave), and was buried in the churchyard at Birchington.

Sea-side burial
Rossetti died, aged 53, while convalescing from a stroke at Birchington-on-Sea in Kent, and was buried in the churchyard there. On his tombstone, designed by Ford Madox Brown, an eloquent epitaph records that he was 'honoured among painters as a painter, and among poets as a poet'.

A Romantic Dreamworld

Rossetti thought of himself as a poet in paint rather than a craftsman. Medieval romance and beautiful women were his favourite subjects, and he painted both with original techniques.

With his strong personality and scant regard for the conventions of the day, Dante Gabriel Rossetti became one of the most individual artists of the 19th century. Even when he was a member of the Pre-Raphaelite Brotherhood, his attitude and technical methods were clearly different from those of his colleagues, who in theory all subscribed to the same ideals.

Rossetti was not a natural craftsman like Millais, to whom painting came almost as easily as breathing, nor did he have the patience of Holman Hunt, whose work owes more to dedication than to inspiration. The young Rossetti, with his lack of a thorough technical training, was in the position of a musician who has great melodies running through his head but has not yet even mastered the scales.

FLAWED MASTERPIECES

His first two major oil paintings, *The Girlhood of Mary Virgin* (p.24) and *The Annunciation* (p.25), are ambitious and original works, but they clearly show his limitations in draughtsmanship and perspective. In *The Annunciation*, for example, there is awkwardness in the tilted effect of the bed on which the Virgin sits and in the positioning of the angel's feet, but it is typical of Rossetti that the

Tate Gallery, London

Bridgeman Art Library

Found (1853)
(left) Rossetti's only attempt at a modern-day morality subject. This elaborate drawing shows a countryman on his way to market recognizing his former beloved, who has now become a prostitute in the city.

The Blue Closet (1857)
(above) This colourful water-colour is typical of Rossetti's work in many ways: in its medieval setting, its musical theme (the meaning of which is obscure) and its bevy of languidly beautiful women.

Fotomas Index

The Preparation for the Passover in the Holy Family (1855)
(right) Rossetti's highly original water-colour technique is clearly demonstrated in this unfinished picture. Mary's blue robe shows how Rossetti used very dry pigment; he has also scraped through it with the 'wrong end' of the brush for texture.

Paolo and Francesca da Rimini (1855)
(below) Although often indolent, Rossetti could work quickly when necessary. This water-colour was painted to help Lizzie Siddal, who had run out of money travelling in France. Madox Brown wrote that Rossetti 'worked day and night, finished it in a week'.

Fotomas Index

Sir Galahad (1857)
(above) Rossetti made several fine illustrations for the Moxon edition of Tennyson's poems, to which Millais and Hunt also contributed.

Tate Gallery, London

Tate Gallery, London

spirit of the work overcomes any technical deficiencies. The daring, almost all white colour scheme and the exquisite expression of the Virgin convey a feeling of elevated purity.

Although Rossetti shared the PRB practice of using family and friends as models for his paintings, he was never interested in the minute particularity of detail that was such a feature of the work of his colleagues. The plain white walls and floor in *The Annunciation* required no elaborate archaeological research and reconstruction, nor the expenditure of a whole day on a few square inches of paint. Rossetti tended to avoid complex backgrounds and he had a positive distaste for landscape, a feature to which Millais, in particular, devoted so much loving attention.

Rossetti also differed from the other Pre-Raphaelites in the large part that water-colour played in his work. It was his favourite medium in the 1850s and he developed a highly original technique, which he applied mainly to subjects from medieval romance. Water-colour had reached its highest development in England in the late 18th and early 19th centuries, but Rossetti's technique was very different from the classic method of applying transparent washes of colour to create what was in effect a tinted drawing. Rossetti applied the paint vigorously, even roughly, producing sparkling, jewel-like effects entirely appropriate to the heraldic trappings he so often portrayed, as in *The Wedding of St George and Princess Sabra* (p.28).

UNUSUAL TECHNIQUES

He made much less distinction than did most artists between water-colour and oils and might use techniques in one medium that would normally seem more appropriate to the other. Often his water-colours look solid and richly textured (he frequently used the paint almost dry, rather than free-flowing – rubbing and scraping at the paper), while his oils sometimes have an almost ethereal delicacy. His friend William Bell Scott (like Rossetti a poet as well as a painter) saw Rossetti at work on *The Girlhood of Mary Virgin* and noted that he was 'painting in oils with water-colour brushes, as thinly as in water-colour'. It is because of these technical idiosyncrasies,

that Rossetti's paintings sometimes look rough or unfinished, but they have an inner glow that is so often missing in the work of artists who achieve an effortless surface polish.

In spite of his hatred of academic discipline, Rossetti was also the outstanding draughtsman among the Pre-Raphaelites. He used drawing not only as a preparation for painting but as a means of expression in its own right, and in the 1850s he was obsessive in the way he drew Lizzie Siddal (or 'Guggums' as he called her) again and again. Madox Brown wrote after a visit to Rossetti in 1855: 'Rossetti showed me a drawer full of "Guggums"; God knows how many. It is like a monomania with him'.

Although he often became totally immersed in certain themes, Rossetti at times showed considerable versatility. His experiments with wall painting at the Oxford Union in 1857 were a dismal failure because he was cavalierly amateurish in technique, but his association with William Morris brought out his talent as a designer of stained glass. And as might be expected of an artist as deeply immersed in literature as Rossetti, he was a brilliant book illustrator, although he did comparatively little work in this field. His illustrations to his sister's poems are among his most charming works.

For the last two decades of his career (he

COMPARISONS

The Femme Fatale

The theme of the femme fatale – an irresistably beautiful woman who brings disaster to the men she entangles – has a long tradition in the history of art. Biblical themes frequently provided the pretext for pictures in which sex appeal played a much greater part than piety. Salome is probably the most famous femme fatale in the Bible: King Herod was so smitten by her that he granted her wish for the head of John the Baptist. Judith used her charms to similar effect but for an arguably more noble purpose. She infiltrated the camp of the Assyrian enemy and killed the enemy general.

Titian (c.1490-1576) Salome
(left) The great Venetian painter Titian excelled in the depiction of sensuous textures. Here the ghastly severed head contrasts strongly with Salome's voluptuous flesh.

Gustav Klimt (1862-1918) Judith
(right) Klimt was one of the supreme exponents of the 'decadence' which was so fashionable around 1900. His Judith looks completely secular – and very seductive.

Bridgeman Art Library

Galleria Doria-Pamphili, Rome

Österreichische Galerie, Salzburg

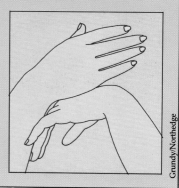

Elegant Hands

To some artists, hands are almost as expressive as faces. Busy society portraitists would often leave most of a picture to assistants but paint the hands as well as the head themselves. The elegant hands of Rossetti's beautiful women help to create his distinctive air of languorous reverie.

Grundy/Northedge

L.S. Lowry Collection on loan to Manchester City Art Gallery

Proserpine (1877)
(above and top right)
This painting is a superb example of the intensity with which Rossetti focuses on various parts of the female body. His friend Theodore Watts-Dunton said that to Rossetti the eyes represented the spiritual part of the face and the mouth the sensuous part. The hands also are deeply expressive.

stopped working in 1878, four years before his death), Rossetti concentrated almost exclusively on paintings of beautiful, sensuous women. Fanny Cornforth was his favourite model for a while and then Janey Morris. With her pouting lips, smouldering eyes and cascades of curls, Janey became in Rossetti's images of her one of the archetypal personifications of the *femme fatale*.

DIVINELY BEAUTIFUL FORMS

Often these paintings have titles in Italian or Latin, but although they may evoke mythological or literary references they have no story-telling element. Rossetti's friend and pupil Edward

Burne-Jones gave a description of his own ideas on painting that could well be applied to Rossetti's late work: 'I mean by a picture a beautiful romantic dream, of something that never was, never will be – in a light better than any that ever shone – in a land no one can define or remember, only desire – and the forms divinely beautiful.'

Rossetti's later work is uneven, partly because of his ill health, partly because he employed assistants, but his finest paintings are amongst the most memorable and enduring images of the 19th century. They were immensely influential and had a whole legion of descendants in the moody, brooding *femmes fatales* who were so much a part of the 'decadent' taste of the 1890s.

The First Anniversary of the Death of Beatrice

Angered and hurt by the abuse hurled at the Pre-Raphaelites, Rossetti stopped exhibiting his work in public, and in the 1850s earned his living painting water-colours for private collectors. This was his most ambitious – and, at two feet wide, his largest – water-colour to date, painted for an Irish businessman named Francis McCracken. Rossetti planned the work carefully, but his vivid reconstruction of a medieval Italian interior was imaginative rather than scrupulously historical; in fact he looked for inspiration to northern European artists such as Albrecht Dürer rather than to the great Italian masters. He spent about nine months working on the painting and McCracken was so pleased that he paid the artist £50 instead of the agreed fee of 35 guineas.

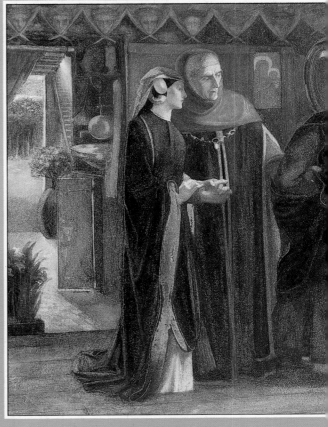

Tender companions
The gently clasped hands of Dante's companions, who come to visit him on the anniversary of his beloved's death, are typical of the tenderness of the painting.

Domestic details
Rossetti's painting is crowded with details, some symbolic, some decorative, and others serving mainly to create a convincing picture of a medieval interior. The water ewer, basin and towel help to evoke an air of everyday domesticity.

Inspiration from the 16th century
(below) This detail from a woodcut of the Birth of Mary by Albrecht Dürer shows Rossetti's source for his still-life detail on the left.

'A thoroughly glorious work – the most perfect piece of Italy I have ever seen in my life.' John Ruskin

Albrecht Dürer/The Life of the Virgin (detail)

Nick Nicholson/The Image Bank

View through a window

(above) Rossetti had no great desire for strict topographical accuracy, but the hazy view seen through Dante's window is strongly reminiscent of Florence's famous river – the Arno.

Ashmolean Museum, Oxford

An early version

Rossetti made this pen-and-ink drawing in 1848-49, five years before the water-colour.

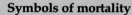

Friends as models

Elizabeth Siddal posed for the woman visitor; her elderly companion was a family servant called Williams.

Symbols of mortality

(right) The still-life details beside the kneeling figure of Dante are symbolic references to the transience of earthly life. They include a lyre and a book, alluding to intellectual pleasures, and a skull – well-recognized as the universal symbol of death.

Berry/Fallon

Gallery

Rossetti was in his early twenties when he first came to prominence as a member of the Pre-Raphaelite Brotherhood. The Girlhood of Mary Virgin and The Annunciation are his key paintings of this period, serious and devout works, but captivating in their youthful ardour and freshness.

After the critical attacks on the PRB,

The Girlhood of Mary Virgin *1849*
32¾" × 25" Tate Gallery, London

This was Rossetti's first important oil painting and his first public success. Modelled by Rossetti's sister and mother, it has great charm in the touching simplicity of the poses and expressions, and is full of symbolic details. Rossetti wrote a sonnet explaining them: the lily in the vase next to the angel, for example, stands for innocence.

Rossetti withdrew from the public art world and for a decade concentrated on water-colours. The Wedding of St George and the Princess Sabra is typical both of his medieval themes and of his love for sparkling colour and elaborate heraldic patterns.

Following the death of his wife, commemorated in Beata Beatrix, Rossetti devoted himself almost exclusively to paintings of beautiful women. His favourite model was Janey Morris whom Rossetti immortalized in a series of powerful images: paintings that are both grand and highly erotic. The most splendid of them all is Astarte Syriaca, the final testimony to Rossetti's lifelong love of female beauty.

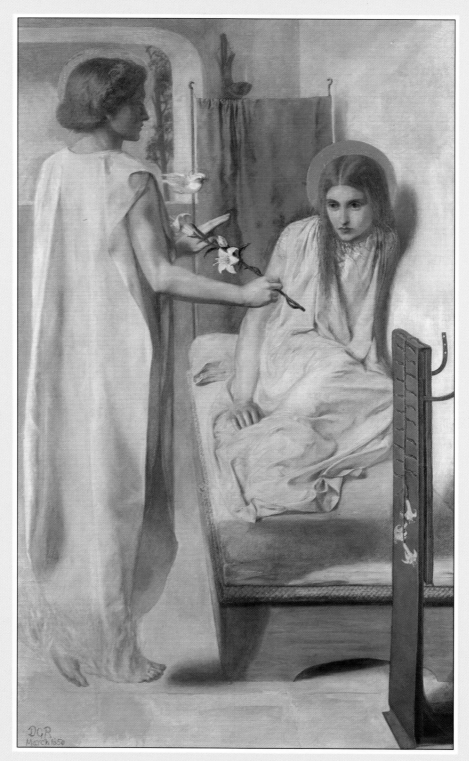

The Annunciation *1850*
28½″ × 16½″
Tate Gallery, London

Rossetti originally planned, but never started, a companion painting on the death of the Virgin, which explains the tall, narrow shape of this picture – together they would have formed a double-painting, or diptych, almost square in shape. The remarkable colour scheme is virtually restricted to white and the three primary colours – blue, red and yellow. Rossetti used several models for the figures of the Virgin and the angel, including his mother and sister Christina.

The First Anniversary of the Death of Beatrice *1853*
16½″ × 24″ Ashmolean Museum, Oxford

Rossetti revered the great Italian poet Dante, after whom he was named, and whose works inspired some of his finest paintings. Here he shows Dante being interrupted by a group of friends while he is drawing an angel, on the anniversary of the death of his beloved Beatrice.

The Wedding of St George and the Princess Sabra *1857*
13½″ × 13½″ Tate Gallery, London

*This glowing water-colour is a fine example of Rossetti's passion for
decorative shapes and patterns. The subject of matrimony was topical,
since Rossetti and his friends Morris and Burne-Jones were all
contemplating marriage. The white bed in the background is the most
direct allusion to marital love. The princess is cutting off a lock of her
hair as a trophy for St George who has just killed the dragon.*

The Tune of Seven Towers *1857*
12½″ × 14½″ Tate Gallery, London

The subject of this melancholy, brooding water-colour is obscure. The figure playing the musical instrument was posed for by Elizabeth Siddal, and Rossetti may have intended the picture to be a commentary on her fragile condition. She has a pilgrim's scallop shell at her throat, perhaps an allusion to her pilgrimage through life or a journey in search of health.

Beata Beatrix *1864-70*
34″ × 26″ Tate Gallery, London

Rossetti painted this intensely spiritual picture as a memorial to his wife, who died in 1862. In it he expresses his love for Lizzie as being a parallel to Dante's idealized love for Beatrice, whose death had left the Italian poet grief-stricken. The bird is a messenger of death, carrying a poppy – a flower that induces sleep.

Monna Vanna *1866*
35″ × 34″ Tate Gallery, London

*One of Rossetti's most sumptuous paintings, this is a portrait of
Alexa Wilding, who regularly modelled for him during this period.
The name 'Monna Vanna' occurs in the poems of both Dante and
Boccaccio, but has no specific connotation here. Rossetti considered
this one of his finest works and he never surpassed it.*

The Bower Meadow *1872*
33½″ × 26½″ City Art Gallery, Manchester

*Music – 'the food of love', as Shakespeare called it – is a common
feature in Rossetti's painting. This is one of his grandest depictions of
the theme, with the counterchanged colouring of the dresses and hair
of the four main figures creating a subtle rhythmic harmony. The
landscape background is unusual for Rossetti.*

Astarte Syriaca *1877*
72″ × 42″ City Art Gallery, Manchester

Rossetti's last masterpiece, this is one of the most majestic images in Victorian art. The model was Janey Morris, portrayed as Astarte, the love goddess of the Ancient Syrians. Rossetti wrote a sonnet describing the painting: Astarte's face embodies 'Love's all-penetrative spell'.

William Morris and Co.

Inspired by the romantic yearnings of Rossetti, William Morris founded a famous company. It was dedicated to the ideals of medieval craftsmanship and to 'decorative, noble, popular art'.

Rossetti is best remembered for his part in the Pre-Raphaelite Brotherhood and for his paintings of exotic *femmes fatales*, but an important part of his life was his association with William Morris (1834-96), the finest artist-craftsman of his time. Today, Morris is most famous for his beautiful wallpaper designs, but in his own day he was renowned as a poet and social reformer, and he was one of the most energetic figures of the Victorian era. His artistic and literary output would have been enough to occupy the lifetimes of 10 ordinary men.

When the Pre-Raphaelite Brotherhood was formed in 1848, William Morris was a schoolboy entering the gates of Marlborough College in Wiltshire. He first learnt of the brotherhood through John Ruskin's *Edinburgh Lectures*, which he read while a student at Oxford in 1854, and enthusiastically narrated to his fellow under-graduate, Edward Burne-Jones (1833-98). Both Morris and Burne-Jones were immediately inspired by the idea of contemporary painters reviving medieval art, and were attracted to the romantic figure of Dante Gabriel Rossetti.

MASTER OF MANY CRAFTS

In 1856, Morris joined Burne-Jones in London to paint under Rossetti's guidance and, in a typical fit of enthusiasm, he declared, 'I want to imitate Gabriel as much as I can'. But he was far too original and versatile a man to remain dominated for long. He mastered a whole range of crafts, including weaving, dyeing, stained glass, block-making, printing and book illumination, and he had a great facility for poetry.

In every sense Morris was a larger-than-life figure. Affectionately known to his friends as Topsy, on account of his uncontrollable mane and beard, he was the constant butt of practical jokes and frequently used to find that his companions had sewn tucks into his waistcoat overnight, knowing that he suffered from a terrible fear of getting fat. His normally jovial nature supported such jokes, but he was also given to explosive fits of rage, when he would hurl sub-standard dinners straight out of the window, break the furniture

into pieces and grind forks into a frenzied knot with his teeth.

After a brief attempt to paint under Rossetti, Morris decided to set up a firm which would specialize in the design and manufacture of decorative and useful goods. Morris, Marshall, Faulkner & Co. (soon known as Morris & Co.), came into being in April 1861, and the founder members, who each put up £1, were Rossetti, Burne-Jones, Ford Madox Brown, Charles Faulkner (an accountant), P. P. Marshall (a surveyor), Philip Webb (an architect), and Morris.

At Oxford, Morris had been greatly influenced

G. F. Watts/William Morris/National Portrait Gallery, London

The philosopher of design
(above) The craftsman William Morris believed that you should 'have nothing in your house that you do not know to be useful and believe to be beautiful'.

A wallpaper masterpiece
(right) Morris's drawing for the Chrysanthemum *wallpaper (1876) shows him using motifs from nature to create a vigorous, closely-patterned design.*

Mary Evans Picture Library

Woodmansterne Ltd./Courtesy of William Morris Gallery, Walthamstow

Burne-Jones/St. Michael & all Angels/Waterford

Bridgeman Art Library

Dante Gabriel Rossetti

Oxford's medieval beauty
(far left) When William Morris went to Oxford in 1853, he found the university town an inspiration. Together with his fellow undergraduate, Edward Burne-Jones, he discovered the beauties of Gothic art, and the medieval colleges and cloisters became their 'chief shrines'.

Stained glass windows
(left) Morris's innovative firm, founded in 1861, specialized in the 'manufactory of all things necessary for the decoration of a house'. In its first years, however, the mainstay of the company was stained glass commissions for small churches.

A bitter quarrel
Rossetti, one of the founder members of the firm, was enraged when Morris decided to dissolve the partnership in 1875. To vent his spleen, he drew this cruel caricature of 'Topsy' Morris tumbling down to Hell.

by Ruskin's notion that medieval art was the expression of a free and happy way of life. Morris & Co. therefore was based on the ideal of a medieval craft guild, where the craftsman designed and executed his own work, and where there was no division of labour into 'intellectual' work and more degrading 'manual' work. The objects were not to be produced by machines and they were to be in a medieval style – a far cry from the tasteless, mass-produced artefacts which cluttered the typical Victorian interior.

In practice, however, much of the company's work was manufactured by outside firms and some machines had to be used for printing and weaving. Workmen had to be employed, for example, to cut wood-blocks for wallpapers, and to cut the lead for glass for stained-glass windows, although Morris supervised these operations.

The firm's prospectus issued in 1861 optimistically offered to provide wall paintings and decoration, stained glass, metal work, jewellery, sculpture, embroidery and furniture, all 'at the smallest possible expense', but in fact the company relied on commissions from Webb to furnish houses, and from church architects for stained glass and for wall- and roof-decorations. Webb himself designed the furniture, much of which was painted by Rossetti, Burne-Jones, Madox Brown and Morris. All five of the artists produced their own designs for the stained glass work which was soon to become the financial backbone of the company.

'Rupes Topseia'/British Museum, London

35

The early 1860s were halcyon days for the group. Evenings would be spent at Morris's 'Red House' at Bexleyheath in Kent, in heated discussion about medieval art, or listening to Morris chanting out his 'grinds', as Rossetti nicknamed his lengthy poems. No one took any interest in the financial affairs of the company, which in its first decade was always on the verge of bankruptcy, although Warrington Taylor, who took over the accounting in 1864, tried to make Morris economize.

BUSINESS BOOMS

In 1870, however, the firm started to receive more commissions, and during the next decade it expanded rapidly as Morris threw himself into experiments with dyeing and weaving. The range of products could now include woollens, silks, chintzes, embroideries, machine-made carpets and the famous wallpapers which allowed Morris to combine his passion for nature with his feeling for pattern and colour. He could be seen shuffling about in his old felt hat and a blue coat barely encompassing his widening girth, stained with indigo from top to toe. The work provided relief from the tension of his unsuccessful marriage to the beautiful Jane Burden, whom Morris idolized from a distance, but could not communicate with.

Rossetti had fallen in love with Jane, and the strains which this caused erupted in 1875 when Morris proposed that Rossetti, and the other founders who had ceased to contribute work, should be retired. Rossetti was not satisfied with the compensation offer and their friendship ended.

Queen Guenevere (1858)
(above) William Morris's only completed oil painting is a portrait of his wife Janey, whom he adored. Melancholy and withdrawn, she was the archetypal Pre-Raphaelite beauty: the novelist Henry James described her as 'a dark silent medieval woman with her medieval toothache'.

Family friends
(right) Morris remained lifelong friends with Burne-Jones, and became devoted to his wife, Georgiana. This 1874 photograph shows the Morris and Burne-Jones families – with Janey, second from the right, in a typically sullen pose.

William Morris Gallery, Walthamstow

William Morris Gallery, Walthamstow

The firm continued to prosper for the rest of Morris's life, but as he became increasingly immersed in socialism and the theories of Karl Marx he could never quite justify its success. Morris believed that good art could not be produced by a society dedicated to profit, and wanted to produce art for the masses; but his products were too expensive for the ordinary working man. And while he railed against the aristocracy and the capitalist system, he was designing wallpaper for Queen Victoria's country seat at Balmoral and ministering to the 'swinish luxury of the rich'.

Nor were Morris' own artistic tastes really suited to the masses. For example, he had a passion for collecting old, rare and expensive illuminated manuscripts. These were the inspiration for his final concern, the setting up of the Kelmscott Press in 1891, to produce beautifully bound and printed editions of classic works, including the famous *Kelmscott Chaucer*. But if he could not reconcile his own ambitions with his achievements, Morris did at least have a tremendous influence on succeeding generations of designers, who adopted his ideals of functionalism combined with good design. His own wallpapers and textiles are still being produced and sold commercially today – by the firm of Sanderson & Co.

Woodpecker tapestry
(above left) Morris soon mastered the arts of dyeing and weaving, and by 1880 was producing subtle and intricate tapestry designs. This tapestry was woven in 1885 on a special loom at the firm's Merton Abbey works.

The Kelmscott Chaucer
(above) In 1891 Morris established the Kelmscott Press, producing hand-printed books with handsome bindings. His most elaborate project was the Kelmscott Chaucer (1896), with its 87 woodcut illustrations by Burne-Jones.

Kelmscott Manor, Oxfordshire

Kelmscott Manor, Oxfordshire
Morris's bedroom at Kelmscott Manor shows the beauty of his interiors. The hangings of the Elizabethan bed were embroidered by his daughter May.

In a year overshadowed by gloom, even the weather seemed doom-laden, as winter stretched into summer. The Church of England saw its foundations undermined by scientists from without and dissenters from within. Foreboding grew when Civil War threatened in America, and Garibaldi and his 'Redshirts' marched through Italy. England, meanwhile, experienced a French invasion scare

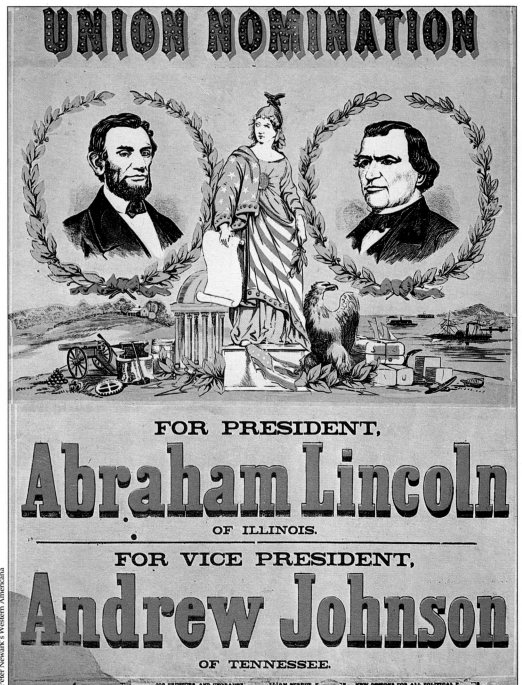

The first typewriter
(above) During the late 1860s, the Americans Christopher Sholes, Carlos Glidden and Samuel Soulé developed the first machine to write faster than the hand – the forerunner of the modern typewriter. The first model went on sale in 1874, manufactured by the gunsmiths Remington and Sons.

Lincoln for President
(left) On 6 November 1860 Abraham Lincoln was elected 16th President of the United States. Despite his optimism, he was powerless to heal the growing divide between North and South. One by one the southern states withdrew from the Union, drawing up the lines for civil war.

The weather was dreadful, especially in London. What the newspapers described as 'the cold, wet, stormy character of this miserable year' lasted from winter into spring and from spring into what should have been summer. Death rates rose significantly and doctors warned that the unending chilling damp was the main reason.

ROSSETTI'S FEARS

Rossetti was sufficiently alarmed to seek out a cottage on the comparatively healthy heights of Hampstead, so that Lizzie should not have to return to the damp, riverside house in Blackfriars when their honeymoon in Paris was over. It was as well that he did, because by the time they got back from Paris in the middle of June the weather was at its worst. June temperatures were the lowest since records had begun and rainfall was three times the average. It was 'a strange season of bluster, menace and gloom', *The Times* concluded, 'and London, we suspect, has had about the worst of it.'

Late in June, the British Association for the Advancement of Science gathered in Oxford to discuss the new and revolutionary ideas of Charles Darwin. A comet blazed in the night sky over central and southern England and the storms continued – well matched by the storms raging inside Oxford's Sheldonian Theatre. There the churchmen did battle with the scientists over Darwin's claim that humanity had not been made in God's image, but had evolved from lower forms of life.

Samuel Wilberforce, Bishop of Oxford and champion of

The birth of competitive skiing
Competitive skiing was made possible in 1860, when the Norwegian Sondre Nordheim first used willow or cane bindings to fasten the boots securely to the skis. Until this time only toestraps were used, which did not allow sufficient control for jumping or turning.

The tram arrives in Britain
(left) In 1860 an American, G.F. Train, opened the first British tramway at Birkenhead, followed by three lines in London. Horse-drawn tram systems had already been introduced in the United States during the 1850s, and spread rapidly in Europe and the US over the next two decades. They were a vast improvement on the old horse-drawn omnibus, since the rails laid in the road allowed a much smoother ride.

Christian orthodoxy, tried to pour scorn on the Darwinian theories, only to find himself outwitted and held up to ridicule. Many who witnessed this defeat thought it signalled the end of traditional religion. Arthur Munby, an extremely devout young man who had been distressed by the whole business, concluded that in future men would have to create God for themselves, 'but of old memories and tottering beliefs'.

AN ATHEIST'S DELIGHT

At this point the Church of England found itself under attack from within. Seven eminent Anglican theologians published a volume called *Essays and Reviews*, which was sufficiently unorthodox to enable hostile critics to claim that the Church was 'honeycombed with disbelief'. 'No fair mind can close this volume,' wrote one atheist reviewer gleefully, 'without feeling it to be at bottom in direct antagonism to the whole system of popular belief.'

Bishop Wilberforce led a campaign to prosecute the contributors to the book. It was no coincidence, he thundered, that so many heresies were being put forward at the same time. They all came from the Devil and they represented 'the first stealing over the sky of the lurid lights which shall be shed profusely around the great Antichrist.' The forces of evil were abroad, 'fluttering in French literature and blaspheming in American spiritualism'.

It was certainly true that spiritualism, like other challenges to traditional Christianity, made great advances in the year 1860.

Archiv für Kunst und Geschichte

Drake's Well
(left) In 1860 Titusville, Pennsylvania was establishing itself as the prosperous centre of the new American oil industry. It was here, on 27 August 1859, that the first successful oil-well had been drilled by Edwin L. Drake (right of picture in top hat).

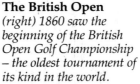

The British Open
(right) 1860 saw the beginning of the British Open Golf Championship – the oldest tournament of its kind in the world. Willie Park was the first Open champion, winning with a 36-hole score of 174. The trophy was a belt of red morocco, richly ornamented with silver plating.

Edimage

Rebellion in Spain
(right) The Carlist rising of 1860 was one of many unsuccessful attempts to overthrow the Spanish government and place Don Carlos and his heirs on the throne. The rebels finally surrendered in their stronghold of Navarre.

Wilkie Collins
(right) In 1860 William Wilkie Collins (1824-89) published The Woman in White, *establishing himself as the master of the mystery story, and the first English novelist to deal with the detection of crime.*

40

The celebrated medium Daniel Home came from America to hold a séance at the home of no less a person than the President of the Board of Trade. An authoritative account was published in the *Cornhill Magazine*: 'I was sitting nearly opposite to Mr Home and I saw his hands disappear from the table and his head vanish into the deep shadow beyond. We watched in profound stillness and saw his figure pass from one side of the window to the other, feet foremost, horizontally in the air.'

'HONEST ABE' ELECTED

Many observers saw more pressing dangers elsewhere. The drift towards civil war in America seemed to be halted with the election of Abraham Lincoln as President. 'For the safety of the Union itself,' declared *The Times* in London, 'we confess we have no fear.' France, however, under the Emperor Napoleon III – nephew of the great Napoleon – seemed to pose a threat. The year before, she had intervened to help the Italians in their struggle for freedom (the *Risorgimento*) against the Austrians.

1860 saw Baribaldi and his Redshirt volunteers almost complete the unification of Italy, but Napoleon III, a cautious man appalled by bloodshed, had already withdrawn his support. This did not avert an invasion scare in England, still haunted by memories of the first Napoleon. There was an enthusiastic response to calls for a volunteer defence force, equipped with new Whitworth guns, but it proved quite unnecessary. In fact, a commercial treaty of lasting importance had been signed by the two countries on 23rd January.

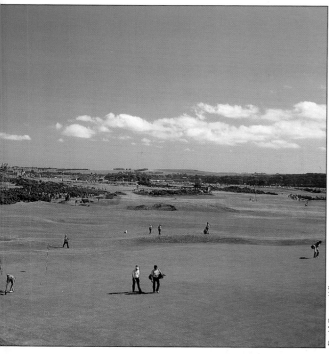

David Cannon/Allsport

Mary Evans Picture Library

Crossing the Australian outback
(below) In 1860 John McDouall Stuart set out from Adelaide, South Australia, in an attempt to cross the Australian continent. After reaching Mount Sturt (now Stuart), the geographical centre of Australia, he was forced to turn back. He set out again the following year and on 25 July 1862 finally reached the Indian Ocean, where the Union Jack was hoisted in celebration.

Peter Newark's Western Americana

Rossetti joined the Artists' Rifle Corps, but never learned to handle the new weapons. He missed most of the training because of his wedding and honeymoon. Other riflemen were more assiduous, and the Queen herself encouraged them by firing the first shot at a rifle competition on Wimbledon Common. A Whitworth rifle was fixed and aimed in advance and the Queen pulled a cord attached to the trigger. 'There was a crack, a hurtling through the air and then a smart thud – Her Majesty's bullet had struck the target within a quarter of an inch of the very centre.'

The weather grew even worse as 'this miserable year' drew to its close. The autumnal gales were particularly ferocious and they blew from the east instead of from the west, so that ships homeward bound in the Atlantic had to contend with fierce headwinds. One was *HMS Hero*, bringing the Prince of Wales back from a successful American tour. She was a fast steamship, able to cross the Atlantic in under 21 days, and she only carried enough coal for that time; 24 days after she left America there was still no sign of her.

HOME IS THE HERO

'Our poor Bertie is still on the Atlantic,' Queen Victoria wrote anxiously, 'detained by very contrary winds. Two powerful steamers have gone out to look for him and bring him in.' The two steamers returned without sighting anything and anxiety grew. When at last *Hero* limped into Plymouth after a passage of 27 days there was great public rejoicing.

Massacre of the Maronites
(below) On 21 June 1860, Der-el-Kamar, a peaceful Maronite village in Lebanon, was attacked by neighbouring Druzes in the centuries-old conflict between Christians and Muslims. In a few days, thousands of Christians were massacred, hundreds of villages burnt to the ground and the Maronite harvests completely destroyed.

Charles Darwin
(above) Following the publication of The Origin of Species *in 1859, Charles Darwin found himself at the centre of a heated debate between scientists and theologians, who saw his revolutionary theory of evolution as a serious threat to the teachings of the church.*

Canada's parliament
(left) In 1860, two years after Queen Victoria selected Ottawa as the capital of Canada, the Prince of Wales laid the cornerstone for the magnificent gothic Parliament Buildings, on the summit of Parliament Hill.

Redon: Self-portrait/Musée d'Orsay, Paris

ODILON REDON

1840-1916

Now regarded as one of the greatest French Symbolist artists, Odilon Redon remained an obscure provincial figure until his mid-40s. During his early years, he pursued a solitary course in opposition to the prevailing naturalism, producing prints and charcoal drawings of macabre and fantastic subjects. It was only in the 1880s, when the reaction to Impressionism became widespread, that Redon received recognition.

For a time, Redon was mistakenly thought of as a literary artist, but as his work became better known, young painters responded to his novel technique and visionary images, and came to regard him as a leader. Contact with these painters, among them Gauguin, had a beneficial effect on Redon, and his late work comprises gloriously colourful pastels and oils which include the flower pieces that won the admiration of Matisse.

43

A Solitary Individualist

A reticent and unassuming man, Redon never achieved widespread popular acclaim, but his highly personal art found its own faithful audience. He is now considered a leading artist of his generation.

Odilon Redon was born in Bordeaux on 20 April 1840, the same year as Claude Monet, but his career and interests are in striking contrast to those of his more famous contemporary. The period of Redon's youth saw the waning of the Romantic movement in France and the triumphant emergence of naturalism in painting leading, in the 1870s, to the formation of the Impressionist group. While the respected traditional forms of mythological and history painting survived, landscape, genre and still-life painting gained tremendous ground, exercising a much greater appeal to the bourgeois public of the mid-19th century. But Redon resisted this movement, and was to criticize naturalists and Impressionists for concentrating on an 'external ideal.' 'Those who remain within these narrow limits commit themselves to an inferior goal', he wrote. The subject of art for Redon was the inner world of the imagination.

It was as a result of his unorthodox approach that Redon remained for so long obscure and unknown. The second son of Bertrand Redon and

Réunion des musées nationaux

Musée d'Orsay, Paris

Zefa

Childhood home
(above) Redon spent his first 11 years with an elderly uncle on the family estate of Peyrelebade, in the Medoc region, where much of his time was spent alone. The area, and the estate, had a particular kind of romantic solitude, portrayed here by the artist, and had a direct influence on forming Redon's artistic imagination.

Bordeaux
(left) In 1851, Redon returned to his place of birth at Bordeaux, where he began his education. It was here that he received his first drawing tuition under a local teacher, Stanislas Gorin, who initiated the boy into the Romantic tradition.

Key Dates

1840 born in Bordeaux
1855 has first drawing lessons with Gorin
1861 meets Clavaud
1863 meets Rodolphe Bresdin in Bordeaux
1870 settles in Paris
1879 produces first album of lithographs, *In Dream*
1880 marries Camille Falte in Paris
1884 exhibits with Société des Artistes Indépendants
1886 participates in last Impressionist exhibition; birth and death of his son Jean
1897 sale of Peyrelebade
1889 birth of Arï
1903 awarded Légion d'Honneur
1916 Redon dies

Marie Guérin, he spent most of his early life in the care of an uncle on the family estate, Peyrelebade, in the Medoc, north of Bordeaux, an area of wild windswept heathland. Even as an established artist he would return to the estate each summer: its melancholy air and memories of his lonely childhood there continued to haunt his work.

Far from Paris, the young Redon became initiated at Bordeaux into Romantic concepts about art which were already old-fashioned. At school he was taught drawing by Stanislas Gorin, a passionate admirer of Delacroix, who instilled Redon with the first principles of Romanticism – that his work should truly express his sensations, and that rules and formulae should be distrusted.

A FORMATIVE INFLUENCE

In 1861, Redon had the good fortune to meet the remarkable botanist Armand Clavaud, who became both a friend and a mentor. Not only did Clavaud's scientific research help to inspire Redon's own imaginative interpretation of nature, but as a scholar of great originality and breadth, Clavaud introduced Redon to philosophy, Hindu poetry, and Greek, medieval and Indian art. Clavaud was also interested in contemporary literature and through him Redon became acquainted with the writings of Edgar Allan Poe and Flaubert, all of which were to have a lasting impression on his own work.

By comparison, Redon's formal training was of little benefit. At his father's insistence, he studied architecture and sculpture, without success, and

Bresdin: The Comedy of Death

New inspiration
(above) Redon spent some time in Bordeaux with the engraver, Rodolphe Bresdin, who was the major inspiration behind the artist's choice of black and white as an expressive medium. Bresdin's works are characterized by strange, sinister images, such as this famous example, The Comedy of Death.

The genius of Delacroix
(left) Through the enthusiasm of Gorin, Redon became an ardent admirer of Delacroix. In the Bordeaux museum where this fragment hangs, Redon made numerous studies of the exhibits. His copy of this work is now our only record of the whole composition.

Delacroix: The Lion Hunt: Musée des Beaux-Arts, Bordeaux

45

then in 1864 he enrolled at the Ecole des Beaux-Arts in Paris under the esteemed academic master Gérôme. For a pupil of Redon's sensibility and originality, the routine of academic instruction was insufferable. He quarrelled with Gérôme and left the Ecole, thereby renouncing his chance of a successful official career.

Redon looked instead to the guidance and instruction of a man who had already turned his back on the official art world and lived the life of a poor bohemian in Bordeaux – Rodolphe Bresdin. Twenty years older than Redon, Bresdin worked in obscurity, producing etchings and lithographs of fantastic and sinister subjects, crowded with detail. These strange and late flowerings of Romanticism drew their inspiration from the prints of Dürer and Rembrandt, and had a powerful effect on the young Redon. He too began to make highly detailed etchings, inspired by Bresdin's images, and like his master chose to depict mysterious, imaginary scenes, turning his back both on academic and naturalistic art.

During the 1860s and 70s Redon worked alone, producing charcoal drawings of astounding

The move to Paris
(below) Redon finally settled in Paris in 1870, after the Franco-Prussian War, although he continued to spend his summers at Peyrelebade. He became a regular visitor at the Salon of Madame de Rayssac where he met artists and writers with similar interests to his own, in particular the great flower painter, Henri Fantin-Latour.

Spectrum

Armand Clavaud

In his account of his own life, *A soi-même*, Redon claimed that to Armand Clavaud's teaching he owed 'the first blossoming of his spirit'. Clavaud was a leading botanist whose evolutionary theories left their mark on Redon's more bizarre work. His broad interests were also a source of inspiration to the artist, ranging from ancient Indian poetry to current avant-garde literature. Through him, Redon came to know the work of Baudelaire, Flaubert and Edgar Allan Poe.

originality. Their strange repertoire of subjects – plants and insects with human faces, severed heads, flying creatures, skeletons and masks – are loosely derived from the art and literature of the Romantic movement, but Redon succeeded, by the simplicity of his design and subtlety of his tonal and textural effects, in giving them a novel and striking resonance.

Even when, in the 1870s, Redon came to live in Paris, he pursued his solitary course. In 1874, the year when the Impressionists first exhibited together, he became a regular visitor to the Salon of Madame de Rayssac, where he met painters and writers older than himself who had known Delacroix and Victor Hugo, the great heroes of Romanticism, and who both shared and helped to foster Redon's ideas about art.

One young man he met there, the flower painter Henry Fantin-Latour, became a firm friend and encouraged Redon to take up lithography as a means of reproducing his drawings and reaching a wider audience. Redon produced his first album of lithographs, *In Dream*, in 1879, and over the next 20 became publicly identified, for better or worse, with the Decadent movement. In 1884, Huysmans published his novel *A Rebours* which was hailed as the manifesto of Decadence. Its hero is a disenchanted aristocrat who retreats from society into a private world of strange and perverse delights. Among the curiosities he collects are Redon's charcoal drawings – which Huysmans himself had just discovered. It was his appearance in this novel that consecrated Redon's reputation as a master of sickness, delirium and depravity.

While his association with the writers of the Decadent and Symbolist movements brought Redon recognition, he always felt that his aims as an artist were misunderstood by them, that they made the error of seeking precise meanings in his work. 'My drawings inspire', he wrote, 'and are not to be defined. They do not determine anything. Like music they take us into the ambiguous world of the indeterminate.'

Artists might have understood him better, but Redon's contacts were largely with writers and intellectuals. In 1884, however, he exhibited with the newly founded Société des Artistes

Roger Viollet

Portrait of Clavaud
(left) Redon became acquainted with Armand Clavaud in Bordeaux in 1861. The artist held the young botanist in such high esteem that he dedicated an album of lithographs – Les Songes, *published in 1891 – to Clavaud. This portrait, the first plate in the album, portrays him as a Christ figure.*

In Dream
(above) Redon produced his first group of lithographs, Dans le Rêve (In Dream), in 1879. This plate from the series, entitled Germination, *has as its theme the creation of man and shows Clavaud's influence in its Hindu references to a Cosmic intelligence and to theories of evolution.*

A happy marriage
(below) Redon met his wife, Camille Falte, at Madame de Rayssac's Salon. They married in 1880 and were, from all accounts, a particularly happy couple. Madame Redon was extremely supportive of her husband, taking care of all their affairs so that he could concentrate on his painting.

Réunion des musées nationaux

years devoted himself almost exclusively to this medium, producing series after series of strange and horrific images. Some are accompanied by mysterious and enigmatic captions of Redon's own making; others, like the masterful *'Death: my irony surpasses all others'* (p.50) from the series *To Gustave Flaubert*, are loosely derived from a wide range of literary sources.

CHANGING FORTUNES

Redon's fortunes underwent a marked change in the 1880s. In 1880 he married Camille Falte, a young woman he had met at Madame de Rayssac's, and the loneliness and isolation of his early life came to an end. In 1881 and 1882, in Paris, he held two small exhibitions of his charcoal drawings which effectively marked the beginning of his public career. Two writers, Emile Hennequin and Joris Karl Huysmans, responded enthusiastically to what they saw and recognized in Redon's macabre drawings links with the new wave of Decadent writers. Through them Redon

Musée d'Orsay, Paris

Portrait of Arï Redon
(below) The death of his first son Jean, in 1886, when he was only 6 months, occurred at a time when Redon was experiencing repeated personal tragedies and the loss affected him deeply. His second son, Arï, was born three years later and his life is associated with happier times. Redon's new optimism is reflected in his more colourful paintings, such as this pastel portrait of a pensive Arï, executed in 1897.

Indépendants, and in 1886, he participated in the last Impressionist exhibition, forming friendships with Seurat and Gauguin. He also showed with Les XX (Les Vingt), a Belgian group who dedicated itself to Symbolist themes.

A BRIGHTER VISION

The effect of these new contacts with painters became evident in the next decade. Redon had always painted a little – landscapes and flower studies – but until about 1890, colour did not play a significant role in his work. The influence of Gauguin changed all that, and in the last years of the 19th century, Redon embarked on a new career as a colourist, producing pastels and paintings of glowing colour which are in dramatic contrast to his sombre 'blacks', as he called his charcoal drawings and lithographs. During the last 20 years

of his life, right up to his death in 1916, Redon created a new oeuvre of joyful optimistic images – portraits, flower pieces, colour fantasies – from which the horrific and macabre obsessions of his earlier work are banished.

The causes of this metamorphosis lie in Redon's private life, which was marked by deep personal sorrows that paved the way for change. After his father's death in 1874, Redon was involved in a long and unhappy family dispute over the inheritance of the family estate; in 1886 his first child, Jean, died in infancy, and over the following years many of his closest friends also died – Hennequin, Bresdin, Clavaud, Mallarmé and Chausson. During the early 1890s, Redon underwent a kind of religious crisis, and in 1894-5 suffered a serious illness, which seems to have marked a watershed in his life. As he recovered, he proceeded to shake off his previous melancholy

The Art Institute of Chicago, Bequest of Kate L. Brewster

Gauguin and the Nabis

In the 1880s, Redon made new contacts with several younger painters. Of these, none had a stronger influence on him than Paul Gauguin. While he gained inspiration from Gauguin's bold use of colour, Redon himself came to be regarded as a champion of Symbolism by the Nabis – the group of artists who followed Gauguin. When Gauguin was away in the South Seas, they turned to Redon for guidance. As Bonnard said; 'Our whole generation is under his charm and benefits from his advice'.

Réunion des Musées Nationaux/©DACS 1988

introspection and religious anxiety. Not unconnected with this resurgence was the sale, in 1897, of Peyrelebade, the scene of his lonely childhood to which he had always remained morbidly attached. This finally severed Redon's links with the past, leaving him free and ready to start afresh. In the words of his second son, Arï, born in 1889: 'With liberty regained, the door was opened wide to life and light. A new and beautiful existence began. After so many dark days it was the dawn of a long and happy period.'

As an artist in his 50s, Redon found himself in the 1890s surrounded by young painters, who unlike many of the artists of his own generation, shared his deepest convictions about art. In particular the group who called themselves the Nabis – Maurice Denis, Paul Sérusier, Bonnard and Vuillard among them – looked to Redon as a leader, who virtually alone had pursued an

Redon in old age
(above) In his later years, Redon's works were shown in Europe, Russia and the United States to enthusiastic public response. However, he remained a most private figure and pursued his own path until his death.

expressive and spiritual art. Gauguin's friend Emile Bernard and the young Matisse were also among his admirers, and the dealers Durand-Ruel and Vollard exhibited his work and helped to encourage a wider acceptance of it. For his part, Redon gained new confidence from this support. He became bolder in his use of colour and more optimistic in his outlook. The macabre subjects of his 'blacks' were replaced by new themes – portraits, nudes, flowers, mythologies – which remain mysterious without being melancholy.

LOYAL PATRONS

Nevertheless, Redon remained a retiring, private figure, and despite the accolades bestowed on him in the early 1900s – in 1903 he was awarded the *Légion d'Honneur*, and the following year was accorded the honour of a room devoted to his work at the Salon d'Automne – his audience remained small. However, it included a group of loyal and dedicated collectors – Gabriel Frizeau, Arthur Fontaine, Gustave Fayet and André Bonger (the brother-in-law of Theo van Gogh) – who commissioned many of the large decorative panels and screens which constitute one of the glories of Redon's late work.

Most notable among the works of Redon's last years are the flower pieces, for the most part painted from the garden flowers which his wife lovingly cut and arranged for him – 'these fragile scented beings, admirable prodigies of light', as he described them. The end of Redon's life was marred by the outbreak of the First World War and his fears for his son Arï, who was serving in the French Army, but his anxiety in no way diminished the radiance of his paintings, which he continued to work on, right up to his death in 1916.

Paul Gauguin
(right) Redon first met Gauguin at the last Impressionist exhibition in 1886, and they became close friends. In marked contrast to the naturalism of his Impressionist colleagues, Gauguin was developing an expressive and decorative style, using bold colours which inspired Redon away from his 'black' works.

Gauguin/Musée d'Orsay, Paris

Homage to Cézanne
(left) Despite its title, this painting by Maurice Denis is actually a homage to Redon by the painters of the Nabis group. He is shown in place of honour at the far left of the canvas, while the other artists pay tribute to him. Vuillard stands beside Redon; Bonnard is shown to the right, with a pipe, and Gauguin is in the foreground next to a still life by Cézanne.

Denis: Homage to Cezanne: Musee d'Orsay, Paris

Flights of Fantasy

In his strange and haunting black and white images and in his dream-like pastels and oils, Redon gives his imagination full rein and probes the mysterious world of man's inner spiritual life.

Kröller-Müller State Museum, Otterlo, Netherlands

Head of a Martyr on a Platter (1877)
(left) The beheading of John the Baptist is a popular subject in Symbolist art, but by showing the severed head in isolation, Redon's image becomes powerful in its own right.

'Death: my irony surpasses all others'
(below) Many of Redon's works were inspired by literary themes, and this famous lithograph, dated 1889, is from the second collection dedicated to Gustave Flaubert. Death is personified in the sinuous form of the femme fatale, which seems to emerge from an indeterminate void.

form to his fantasies. The repertoire of Redon's 'blacks' has its origin in Romantic literature and painting, as well as in the more popular illustration of the period. The artists to whom he looked for inspiration were Eugène Delacroix – the leading painter of the Romantic movement in France – and Gustave Moreau, who like Redon resisted the vogue for naturalism, and produced very personal interpretations of mythological subjects.

Yet the power of Redon's images is not due to their strange and macabre subject matter alone. Indeed much of his imagery is, for its date, curiously old-fashioned and unoriginal. They depend for their influence on the great range of visual effects of which Redon was a master. Even when limited to a monochrome palette, he exploited to the full the effects of line, texture, and tone to impart resonance and mystery to his subjects. It is in his technical virtuosity in rendering his startling images that Redon was in advance of his time. Even before he came to use colour, Redon's work achieved a 'painterly' depth of tone and expression.

The transition to colour saw a parallel transition to new, optimistic themes. 'If the art of an artist is

The most remarkable feature of Redon's work as an artist was the transition in the 1890s from nightmarish visions, worked in monochrome, to vividly coloured pastels and oils which in theme and conception are joyful affirmations of life.

A more complete metamorphosis is hard to imagine, and yet the two phases of Redon's work, the macabre and the optimistic, are linked by a common concern with the inner spiritual life. Throughout his career Redon sought to express in his work the mysterious invisible world that exists alongside the natural physical world. 'I have placed here', he wrote, 'a little door opening on to the mysterious.' It is because of this that, even before the Symbolist movement began, Redon was a Symbolist, using the imagery of his art to suggest and evoke the world of the imagination.

The real roots of Redon's art lie in his most personal experience, and particularly in the memories of his lonely childhood spent at the family estate, Peyrelebade. He later confessed, 'it was necessary there to fill one's imagination with the unlikely, for into this exile one had to put something.'

But while his melancholy and nervous childhood provided the mainspring for his art, Redon still needed to draw on other sources to give

the song of his life', he wrote, 'I must have sounded the note of gaiety in colour.' The change is reflected in his choice of mythological subjects – *Pegasus Triumphant* (below) instead of *Pegasus Chained*, and the recurring theme of the sun chariot of Apollo, the begetter of light and colour.

THE SYMBOL OF CONTEMPLATION

But at the same time, Redon continued to represent the inner life. The mood, however, was contemplative and assured. Among the colour works are numerous religious subjects – including *St Sebastian* (p.55) – in which the richness and originality of the colour effects evoke a strange mystical quality. A favourite device of Redon's is the head with closed eyes, the type of the visionary and a symbol of contemplation. It was the subject of one of his early oils, *Closed Eyes* (left), and the motif recurs in his treatments of Orpheus, Ophelia and various religious themes. With eyes closed to

Réunion des musées nationaux

Musée d'Orsay, Paris

Wild Flowers in a Long-necked Vase
(below) Redon always regarded Nature as his model, and in his old age, flowers provided the subject for a large number of his paintings. Sometimes these were highly stylized, or imaginary blooms, and sometimes, as here, straightforward, naturalistic depictions of flowers from his garden in the Paris suburb of Bièvres.

Closed Eyes (1890)
(above) This quiet work is one of Redon's first oils to treat the subject of the inner life and marks a turning point in his career. Modelled on Redon's wife, the head is a metaphor for spiritual awareness: the lighting, the closed eyes and the tranquil expression all suggest a spiritual state of mind.

Pegasus Triumphant
(below) Black had been 'the most essential of all colours' for Redon – 'an agent of the spirit', but following the transition to colour, his works achieved a new confidence after 1900. Painted in 1907, this is one of several joyous mythological works: its strong colouring suggests the violence of the struggle.

Kröller-Müller State Museum, Otterlo, Netherlands

Musée d'Orsay, Paris

Giraudon

the material world, the visionary sees into himself and the spiritual world. In the pastel of *Ophelia Among the Flowers* (pp.58-9), the drowning heroine from Shakespeare's *Hamlet* seems rather to be in a trance or dream, and the flowers which surround her seem to be the creations of her vision, so fantastic and unreal do they appear.

Flowers often appear in Redon's late works surrounding and enveloping figures like a halo of colour and light. Sometimes the figures, like the flowers, are gorgeous, imaginary apparitions. Sometimes, as in the *Portrait of Violette Heymann* (opposite) the flowers adorn real people and create a magical environment for them. As he had previously conceived fantastic monsters, he now improvised brilliantly coloured shapes and forms, abstract creations of extraordinary variety which evoke a flora more marvellous than any known on earth. In these late works, Redon reached a pinnacle of technical virtuosity, bringing together a dazzling array of graphic and painterly effects and creating luminous colour harmonies.

Redon is at his most abstract in his large pastels and screens, in which, by virtue of their scale, his designs take on an independent, decorative existence. But elsewhere in his late work, Redon shows a new objectivity, a reconciliation with the physical world. Nowhere is this more evident than in the images of *Birth of Venus* (p.62) or *Pandora*, mythological themes which are the pretext for beautiful female nudes – images of sensual delight replacing the earlier type of the femme fatale.

There are also exquisite still-lifes, pictures of shells, butterflies and above all flowers, in which Redon represents real things without distortion. The last of the flower pieces are the most simple and direct – vases of recognizable garden flowers placed centrally within the picture, against an empty background. Nevertheless they are far from simple in their effect. In these late works Redon seems to reveal to us the essential nature of the flowers, in the same way that he laid bare the mysteries of the spirit.

Réunion des musées nationaux

Louvre, Paris

COMPARISONS

Portraits of Women with Flowers

Particularly characteristic of Redon's work is the motif of the beautiful woman surrounded by flowers. She is most frequently shown in profile, recalling the exquisite female portraits of Italian 15th-century painting, and one such picture, Pisanello's *Portrait of a Princess of the d'Este Family*, which entered the Louvre in 1893, may have first suggested the combination of an idealized profile with a background of flowers. Redon also had the example of Gauguin at hand, who, in various portraits of the 1880s, had placed his sitters against a flowered background, as if against a patterned wallpaper or fabric.

Paul Gauguin (1848-1903) **La Belle Angèle** (right) *One of the greatest of the French Post-Impressionist painters, Gauguin spent long periods at Pont-Aven in Brittany, and the Breton peasants became a frequent subject in his work. In this portrait of Mme Angèle Satre, dated 1889, the flowers form part of a decorative backdrop which shows the artist's love of the exotic, and his increasing preoccupation with Symbolism.*

Réunion des musées nationaux

Pisanello (c.1395-1455/6) **Portrait of a Princess of the d'Este Family**
(above) *A northern Italian painter, Pisanello worked in the contemporary International Gothic style and was patronized by numerous Italian courts, including those of the celebrated d'Este and Gonzaga families. Pisanello's paintings are notable for their richness of colour and texture and for their delicately observed naturalistic detail. Here the likeness of the unknown Princess is set against a purely decorative background of flowers and butterflies – a frequent device of the northern Italian school.*

Musée d'Orsay, Paris

LOOKING AT A MASTERPIECE

Portrait of Violette Heymann

Looking back on his career as an artist, Redon claimed that his originality consisted of putting 'the logic of the visible at the service of the invisible', and in his diary he noted Corot's advice to him: 'Beside a certainty, place an uncertainty.' The remarkable *Portrait of Violette Heymann* of 1909 depends for its power on the juxtaposition of the known and the unknown: the finely observed and delicately executed portrait of the young woman, surrounded by an aura of fantastic blooms. The firmly drawn head and contemporary dress of the girl speak of the real world of bourgeois French society at the turn of the century, while the multi-coloured aura is the creation of the imagination, magical and dream-like. Nevertheless, there is no discordance between the two. They are linked by technique, by the unique and beautiful use of pastel that constitutes Redon's handwriting as an artist.

TRADEMARKS

Luminous Colour

In his pastels and oils, Redon seems to have delighted in the luminosity of colour. But colour also had an evocative power for him and he used his luminous blues and mauves to give a mysterious, other-worldly quality to his pictures.

A brilliant subtlety
(left and detail above) One of the artist's most exquisite pastels, this picture displays Redon's dazzling virtuosity and subtlety of touch: the soft smudged treatment of the dress and the hair, the sharp linear drawing of the sleeve and the chair, dense scribbles of lines, and dots of bright colour. Throughout the picture — and especially amongst the fantastic colouring of the imaginary flowers — areas of the pale paper ground show through, giving the effect of another colour and imparting a freshness to the whole.

The Cleveland Museum of Art, Hinman B. Hurlbut Collection

Gallery

Redon did not turn from black and white work to pastels and oils until he was in his 50s, when he revealed his marvellous powers as a colourist. He revelled in handling his new materials and, in 1903, wrote that painting depends above all on 'a gift of delicious sensuality, which can with a little of the most simple liquid substance

Orpheus *c.1903*
27½″ × 22¼″ Cleveland Museum of Art

In Greek legend, Orpheus was a famous poet and musician. After failing to rescue his wife Eurydice from Hades, he came to despise all women and was torn to pieces by the women of Ciconia in Thrace. Redon shows his severed head seemingly floating on his lyre, which he played with incomparable skill. The picture avoids the gruesome aspects of the legend and is a meditation on the poet's death rather than an illustration of the story.

Gift from J. H. Wade

reconstitute or amplify life, leave its imprint on a surface, from which will emerge a human presence, the supreme irradiation of the spirit'.

With the exception of his flower pieces, Redon was little concerned with depicting the world of external reality. He was sometimes inspired by the traditional themes of religion and mythology, as in St Sebastian and Birth of Venus, but the subjects are filtered through his extraordinary imagination to produce something entirely novel. Most of his paintings, however, defy categorization, and in such works as Mystery and Homage to Leonardo da Vinci he created a unique world of poetic fantasy.

Alain Danvers

Saint Sebastian *c.1900-10*
26¾″ × 20¾″ Musée des Beaux-Arts, Bordeaux

Saint Sebastian was an early Christian martyr who was shot with arrows by his executioners. The subject often served more as a pretext for painting beautiful male nudes than as a vehicle for intense religious expression, but Redon creates a genuinely tragic and mystical feeling with his sparse and stormy setting and fantastic colouring. Redon often painted religious subjects, but kept his own religious convictions private.

Mystery *c.1905-07*
28¾″ × 21¼″ Phillips Collection, Washington

*The enigmatic and contemplative figure has a Christ-like appearance,
but Redon makes nothing specific, leaving the spectator free to read
whatever he wants into the painting. Redon frequently combined
figures with flowers, but it is often difficult to know whether they are
mainly decorative or have some deeper significance.*

Head of Christ and Snake *1907*
26″ × 20″ Private Collection

*Bizarre combinations of human and animal forms are a feature of
Redon's work, but few are as intriguing as this one. In orthodox
Christian thought, the snake is a symbol of evil, but it has also been
used to signify fertility, wisdom and the power to heal. Redon was
possibly inspired by Hindu philosophy, in which he had a great interest.*

Ophelia among the Flowers *1905-08*
25¼″ × 35¾″ National Gallery, London

The tragic death of the heroine of Shakespeare's
Hamlet was a popular subject with painters in
the 19th century, but Redon's dreamlike
evocation of the theme is a world away from the
kind of detailed illustration of the story found
most memorably in Millais' celebrated picture
in the Tate Gallery, London. The flowers dominate
the composition, and in fact the picture began by
representing a vase of flowers, but Redon
imaginatively altered it as he worked. If the
picture is viewed on its side (with what is now
the right-hand side at the bottom), the suggestion
of a vase and a table top emerge from the
'landscape' background.

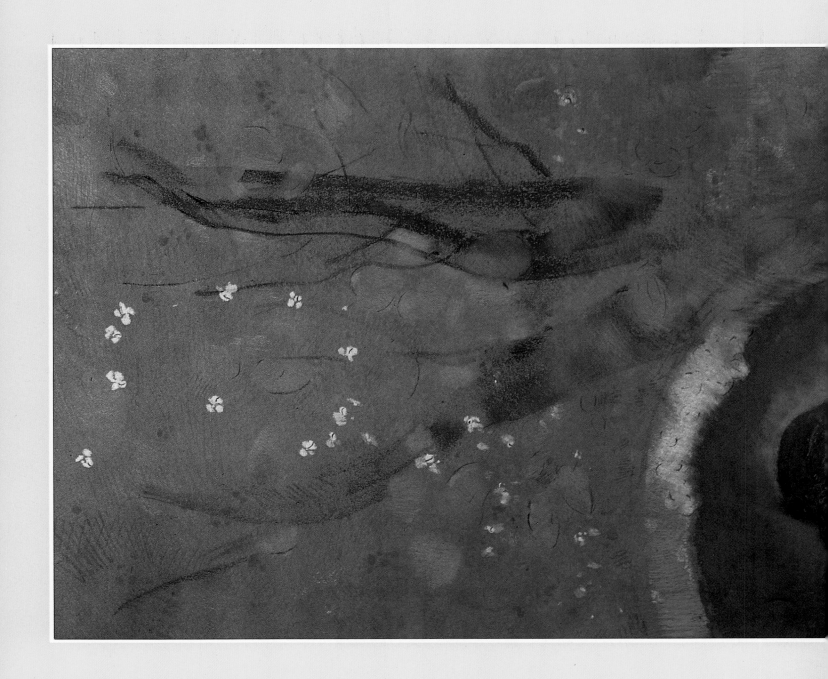

Homage to Leonardo da Vinci 1908
57" × 24¾" Stedelijk Museum, Amsterdam

The title at first seems rather perplexing, but is explained by the fact that Redon was paying homage to an artist, who like himself, had passionately explored the beauty of nature. In his youth Redon made drawings after Leonardo, and the female head here is based on that of the Virgin in Leonardo's Virgin and Child with St Anne.

Giraudon

Birth of Venus *c.1910*
32½″ × 25¼″ Musée du Petit Palais, Paris

*Late in life Redon did a series of pictures on mythological themes that
featured the female nude. The subjects were appropriate to the
sensuousness of his technique, but Redon used them as springboards
for his imagination rather than as stories to be depicted in detail.
Venus was born of the sea and floated ashore on a scallop shell.*

Roger and Angelica *c.1910*
36″ × 28″ Collection, The Museum of Modern Art, New York

The subject is taken from the epic Orlando Furioso *by the Italian
Renaissance poet Ludovico Ariosto. The beautiful princess Angelica is
chained to a rock and is about to be attacked by a sea monster when
she is rescued by the knight Ruggiero (Roger). However, here the
figures are almost lost in the dazzling whirl of colour.*

Bouquet of Flowers *c.1910-12*
15¾″ × 12½″ Kroller-Muller Museum, Otterlo

*Comparing this picture with the one on the opposite page shows how
subtly Redon could vary his approach to depicting a simple vase of
flowers, even when they both have a plain background with no
suggestion of a spatial setting. Here the more richly applied paint
gives the flowers a greater feeling of physical substance.*

Flowers in a Turquoise Vase *1910-12*
25½″ × 19¾″ Private Collection

*Redon was one of the greatest of all flower painters, delighting
particularly in the infinitely variegated colours of the blooms. Here he
shows his remarkable deftness in handling oil paint, applying it thinly
so that the canvas shows through in places and keeping the colours
pure and unmixed so that they retain maximum freshness.*

65

Archiv für Kunst und Geschichte

Red Sphinx *1910-12*
24″ × 19½″ Private Collection

*The sphinx – a monster with the body of a lion and a human head –
featured in Egyptian and Greek mythology as a symbol of power,
vigilance and lust, and a proposer of riddles. Redon's vaguely
delineated painting resists specific analysis; rather, it conveys a
sense of mystery appropriate to this fabulous enigmatic beast.*

The Evocation of the Butterflies *1910-12*
21¾″ × 16¼″ Detroit Institute of Arts

*This joyous work is one of Redon's boldest and most uninhibited
demonstrations of his power and originality as a colourist. The
butterfly is a symbol of the soul leaving the body or of the resurrected
soul, but no such specific meaning can be read into the picture,
which above all is concerned with the sensuous beauty of paint.*

The Symbolist Movement

The Symbolists rebelled against the tradition of naturalism in painting and sought to convey feeling and emotions through their innovative use of colour and esoteric symbols.

Symbolism was not a style but a series of aesthetic attitudes which have underwritten the major developments of 20th-century art. It came about as a reaction to the prevailing fashion for naturalism which, it was increasingly felt, had debased art through its insistence on depicting the visible world at the expense of idealism.

Jean Moréas was the first to christen this disillusionment. 'Symbolist' art, he announced in his manifesto published in *Le Figaro Littéraire* in 1886, would be based on ideas presented as analogies. Moréas was a French poet and Symbolism was initially a literary concept. However, its emphasis on emotional expression inevitably led to links with artists in other fields. Among its leaders were the poets Stéphane Mallarmé and Paul Verlaine who had recognized the affinity between their ideals and music; and J. K. Huysmans, like other Symbolist writers, sought out painters who shared his outlook.

Munch: Art Institute of Chicago

Boldini/Musée d'Orsay, Paris/Réunion des Musées Nationaux/©DACS 1988

Portrait of a Symbolist
Stéphane Mallarmé was the main poet of the Symbolist movement and regular meetings were held at his flat. His writing contained the mystery and metaphor the movement revered.

The cult of the dandy
(right) Count Robert de Montesquiou was an aesthete and model for des Esseintes, the central character of J. K. Huysmans' Symbolist novel A Rebours *(Against Nature).*

Huysmans' book, *A Rebours (Against Nature)*, appeared in 1884 and is a significant work in the history of Symbolism. For it not only defined certain characteristics of the Symbolist aesthetic – its hero, des Esseintes, personified Baudelaire's cult of the decadent dandy – it also pointed to recent forerunners of Symbolist concerns. The theory of correspondences between experiences of nature and states of mind, formed by the poet and critic Charles Baudelaire, was very inspirational. Feeling and not description was paramount in a work of art, which had to act as an equivalent of that experience. In this abstract fashion, the artist could suggest a more authentic picture than straightforward depiction. Above all, Huysmans drew attention to painters like Redon and Gustave Moreau who seemed to touch on this hidden reality.

Moreau had been exhibiting intermittently since the 1860s, when he stood in opposition to the increasingly pervasive tide of naturalism. By developing the academic tradition of romantic idealism, he transformed his mythical subject matter into intense metaphors that pointed to the individual psyche. Thus, his pictures were primarily ideas dressed in exotic clothes and populated with fantasy figures, regardless of historical epochs.

A new approach
(below) Gauguin's Vision after the Sermon *made him a new Symbolist hero. His use of non-naturalistic colour and outline was a deliberate attempt to simplify art and stress the expressive and abstract elements of line, form and colour.*

Firing the imagination
(right) 'I believe only what I do not see and wholly in what I feel', wrote Gustave Moreau and The Apparition *is a perfect example of his haunting images which so captured the imagination of Symbolists like Huysmans.*

Archiv für Kunst und Geschichte

Musée d'Orsay, Paris

National Gallery of Scotland, Edinburgh

By the mid-1880s, Moreau was considered in tune with emergent Symbolist attitudes. The artist had once stated that 'I believe only in what I do not see and wholly in what I feel'. In his paintings, Moreau seemed to dream with his eyes open, to explore the parallel but self-contained world of the subconscious.

Artists and writers began to work together on the production of periodicals which spread their ideas through Europe and to America. *La Revue Blanche* was an important example, a review which encouraged artistic collaborations and, consequently, helped the careers of those artists who illustrated its pages – Munch's famous lithograph, *The Scream*, appeared there in 1895.

THE REAL WORLD UNVEILED

For the Symbolists, art had an immense power because it could reveal the 'real world' unclouded by the world of perceived phenomena which they saw as illusory. Art was something independent, obeying new rules; and became perhaps superior

Hans Hinz

Kunstmuseum, Basle

The Island of the Dead
(above) Böcklin intended this to be 'a picture for dreaming over': it does not depict a specific place or subject. The title was coined by a dealer who was inspired by its imagery of death.

The Poor Fisherman
The Symbolists admired the enigmatic quality and the melancholy mood of Puvis de Chavannes' pictures (see right), although his work is stylistically closer to French Academic art.

to everyday life. What is more, the artist was imbued with a comparably special, autonomous status apart from less sensitive mortals with whom he could not be expected to communicate. The different ways in which the theorists tackled their ambitious task show that Symbolism was not a fixed style. One important approach was adopted by Paul Gauguin who advocated a simplified art that stressed the expressive abstract elements of line, form, and colour as early as 1888.

Yet Gauguin's was not the only approach. The theorist Joséphin Péladan insisted that subject matter was crucial, as long as it was not trivial or vulgar: it had to transcend its own time. To guide artists, he published a set of rules which governed his Salon de la Rose + Croix when it first opened at Durand-Ruel's gallery in 1892. His stated aim was to 'ruin realism', and work was accepted if the subject was appropriate, even though the execution was imperfect: the *idea* was paramount. Among the recommended subjects were Catholic dogma, the interpretation of 'Oriental theogonies except those of the yellow races', allegory, and the nude made sublime. However, Symbolism never promoted non-representational art.

This inward investigation had a mystical, almost religious aspect. Indeed, Munch said of his great programme, 'People will understand the

I Lock the Door upon Myself
(left) In Khnopff's haunting portrait of his sister, the presence of a bust of Hermes – who guides the souls of the dead to the underworld – and the three lilies that bloom and wither in the foreground, suggest death and oblivion.

The Symbolist Salon
(right) In 1892 Joséphin Péladan launched his Salon de la Rose + Croix. He chose the title to reflect his Rosicrucian beliefs, and his set of rules stated that the Salon would promote the Catholic ideal, mysticism and allegory in art.

Artothek

Neue Pinakothek, Munich

Réunion des musées nationaux

Musée d'Orsay, Paris

Bulloz

sacredness of it, and will take off their hats as if 'hey were in church'; and Van Gogh, who saw art as a form of redemption, wrote that masterpieces 'lead to God'. These religious overtones for their secular work echo the spiritual quest of Symbolism. The search for new ways to convey underlying verities also reflects Nietzsche's proclamation in 1882 of 'the greatest modern event, that God is dead'. Artists seemed to attempt to fill this new void through art.

THE FORMATION OF THE NABIS

Symbolism claimed its adherents as if it were a religious fraternity too. Those inspired by Gauguin's radical 'synthetist' theories became the Nabis, taking their name from the Hebrew word for prophet. They met on Saturdays and had nicknames; Bonnard was a member, as was Denis, known as *le nabi aux belles icônes*. Péladan formed a club, of which he was high priest, which was fascinated by occultism and Roman Catholic ceremony, while Huysmans was for a time linked to the notorious Satanist, Abbé Boullan.

One other important theme was that of the femme fatale, the haunting, beguiling predator of the human spirit. A source for this interest lies in the influential music of Richard Wagner, once more indicating the powerful cross-fertilization of the arts. Kundry from *Parsifal* recurs in paintings, often in the guise of Salome engaged in her intoxicating dance. She represented for the (mostly male) writers, and painters the insatiable and consuming human passions; and she reappears, in different forms, in the social dramas of Ibsen and Wedekind, as well as in the paintings of artists as different as Moreau, Munch and Dante Gabriel Rossetti. Indeed, the fifteen years of true

Symbolist ascendancy were also the period of intense psychological study.

The great decade of Symbolist art was the 1890s; and its impact was widespread, touching every branch of the arts. It especially reinvigorated the decorative and applied arts through the growing interest in abstract elements. Although Symbolist attitudes were exhausted as a thriving artistic idiom by the early 1900s, their influence has been felt throughout this century.

Above all, Symbolist ideas released new possibilities. The emergence of non-representational art in the new century was a confirmation of Symbolist painters' concern for an independent art of evocation through line, colour and form. It is no coincidence that the key figures of true abstraction, Kandinsky, Malevich and Mondrian, had their artistic roots in the 19th-century Symbolist movement.

The recognition finally won by Redon in his old age coincided with the eventual achievement of the Franco-British *Entente Cordiale*. Meanwhile Russia was attacked by Japan, suffered unexpected defeats and almost blundered into a war with Britain through naval incompetence.

In 1904, the annual Salon d'Automne allocated a whole room to Redon's work. While the artist was already assured of success and security, his native country, France, was feeling less confident. She seemed likely to lose the friendship of Russia, since she was unwilling to assist her ally in the looming Far Eastern crisis. Her only alternative seemed to be an understanding with Britain, the colonial rival who had humiliated France by ousting her from Egypt and the Sudan. Months of negotiations culminated in the *Entente Cordiale* – a set of colonial agreements, ranging from Newfoundland to Siam and the New Hebrides, that cleared up all the differences between the two powers. The lynch-pin of the *Entente* was a piece of colonial horse-trading: France endorsed Britain's position in Egypt in return for a free hand in Morocco. As a

National Portrait Gallery, London

Joseph Conrad
(left) Born in Poland in 1857, Conrad went to sea at the age of 17, spending the next 22 years as a merchant seaman. His duties took him to a variety of places which later became settings for his most famous stories. Nostromo (1904) is a tale of corruption and revolution in a South American republic. As in all his best works, the central character has a fatal flaw which Conrad probes with relentless psychological insight.

Jean-Loup Charmet

Bibliothèque Nationale

L'Assiette au Beurre

N° 119
Juillet 1903

40 Centimes

LOUBET A LONDON

Par GALANIS et D'OSTOYA

Anglo-French amity
(left) In 1903, Edward VII made a state visit to Paris. His popularity paved the way for the visit of the French President, Loubet, accompanied by his foreign minister Delcassé, who began talks with his opposite number, Lord Landsdowne. The Anglo-French entente, signed in April 1904, organized British and French spheres of influence in North Africa and prevented involvement on opposite sides in the Russo-Japanese War.

result, in October 1904 France and Spain were able to sign an agreement visualizing the partition of Morocco. The *Entente* was a turning-point which apparently committed neither side to very much; yet it led on to 'military conversations' in 1906, and ultimately to joint involvement in the First World War.

WAR IN THE EAST

The Russo-Japanese War began in February 1904 with a Japanese surprise attack on Port Arthur, but the conflict was not in itself unexpected. Russia and Japan were rivals for colonialist 'influence' in Manchuria and Korea, and Russia had wilfully rebuffed all Japanese attempts to negotiate. This was done partly from arrogant over-confidence and partly from a belief that a war might solve Russia's internal problems. Vyacheslav Plehve, the viciously reactionary Minister of the Interior, argued that 'a short, victorious war would stem the tide of revolution'. Instead the Japanese army defeated the Russians and bottled up their Far Eastern navy in besieged Port Arthur. These humiliations intensified unrest in Russia, where Plehve was assassinated in July and demands for political and economic rights multiplied. In this way, the stage was set for the upheavals of 1905.

Russian incompetence became embarrassingly obvious in October 1904, when the Baltic Fleet was ordered to the Far East and fired on British trawlers in the belief that they were Japanese torpedo boats. Two British fishermen were killed in the Dogger Bank incident, but war was averted when,

敵旗艦自觸水雷沈没麻可露
夫提督以下来員八百葬魚腹

Victoria & Albert Museum, London

Michael Holford

Russian disaster
(left) By 1904, Russian and Japanese imperialist ambitions had reached a deadlock. On 8 February, Admiral Togo sailed for Port Arthur, China, torpedoed two Russian battleships and blockaded the rest of the fleet. On 13 April, he succeeded in blowing up the Russian flagship, the Petropavlosk, *drowning Admiral Makarov and 800 crew, an event commemorated here by Kokyo, a contemporary Japanese war artist.*

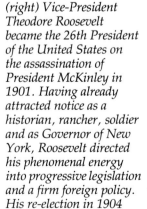

Tibetan debâcle
(left) Lord Curzon, the Indian Viceroy, convinced of Russian infiltration into Tibet, urged the Foreign Office to sanction an expedition. On 11 December 1903, an army under Colonel Francis Younghusband entered the country, travelling for many months in hostile conditions. By the time they reached Lhasa the following August, nearly 3,000 Tibetans had been killed, and not one Russian was found in the Tibetan capital.

Jean-Loup Charmet

Roosevelt re-elected
(right) Vice-President Theodore Roosevelt became the 26th President of the United States on the assassination of President McKinley in 1901. Having already attracted notice as a historian, rancher, soldier and as Governor of New York, Roosevelt directed his phenomenal energy into progressive legislation and a firm foreign policy. His re-election in 1904 with a larger majority than his predecessor testified to his popularity.

Archiv für Kunst und Geschichte

conscious of their weakness, the Russians agreed to submit the affair to arbitration and pay compensation.

The year 1904 was notable in the history of drama. Anton Chekhov, whose *The Cherry Orchard* was given its first production by the Moscow Art Theatre, died later in the year. In London, *Peter Pan*, J. M. Barrie's classic fantasy for children, made its first appearance, while Lady Gregory and W. B. Yeats founded the famous Abbey Theatre in Dublin, one of the landmarks in the Irish literary and national revival. The dramatist J. M. Synge became a director of the theatre which staged his new one-act play *Riders to the Sea* that year.

In France, there was fierce opposition to government measures to break the Catholic Church's hold on education; this was to lead to the separation of Church and State in 1905.

A general strike paralyzed Italy and the great Herero uprising challenged German colonial rule in South-West Africa; Colonel Francis Younghusband led a British expedition to Lhasa, massacred a few hundred Tibetans, and imposed a treaty on the Dalai Lama. 'Teddy' Roosevelt was elected for a second term as US president, and the New York subway train system was opened. C. R. Rolls and Co. merged with Royce Ltd to form the Rolls-Royce company. Puccini's opera *Madame Butterfly* failed badly, underwent revision, and turned into a triumph; and the composer Dvořák died. Several distinguished novels were published, including Joseph Conrad's *Nostromo* and Henry James's *The Golden Bowl* while an entirely new age was foreshadowed by the birth of two novelists of 20th-century disillusion, Graham Greene and Christopher Isherwood.

Puccini's *Madame Butterfly*
(below) The audience that greeted the La Scala première of Puccini's great tragic opera on 17 February 1904 was extraordinarily hostile, although many people have since suspected deliberate sabotage.

The Herero uprising
(above) The Germans joined the 'scramble for Africa' between 1883 and 1885, acquiring four colonies, including South West Africa (Namibia). Their murderous campaign and subsequent occupation resulted in a revolt of the Herero tribe, which was brutally repressed in 1904.

GUSTAV KLIMT

1862-1918

The most famous painter of turn-of-the-century Vienna, Gustav Klimt was born in the Austrian capital in 1862. His goldsmith father sent him to the School of Applied Arts, where he proved a highly successful student. By the time he was in his mid-thirties, Klimt had completed a number of prestigious decorative schemes in public buildings in Vienna and was on his way to becoming a pillar of the Austrian establishment.

All this changed in the 1890s, when Klimt's involvement with the Viennese Secession, followed by scandal over his ceiling paintings for Vienna University, cast him in the role of leader of the city's artistic avant-garde. Klimt's paintings are like highly-decorated precious objects, but beneath their jewelled surfaces lies an erotic content of a neurotic and often morbid nature that many of his contemporaries found deeply shocking.

The Reticent Viennese

Klimt lived and worked all his life in his native Vienna where his work often provoked controversy. Warm and communicative with friends, he shunned publicity and talked little about his work.

Gustav Klimt was born in the Imperial city of Vienna on 14 July 1862. His father Ernst was an engraver and goldsmith of Bohemian origin. Gustav was the eldest of seven children in what was an unusually talented family. His brother Georg followed their father's trade and became a goldsmith, and his brother Ernst also showed a precocious talent for drawing and painting. When they were in their early teens, Gustav and Ernst were sent to the newly established School of Applied Arts (the *Kunstgewerbeschule*) in Vienna.

The art education that the brothers received from Professor Ferdinand Laufberger was remarkably wide-ranging. They learnt to master not only oil painting, but mosaic and fresco techniques as well. In their spare time, they earned extra money by drawing portraits from photographs, which perfected their ability to capture accurate likenesses of people. They also struck up a friendship with their fellow student Franz Matsch, and the trio so impressed the professor with their combined talents that he recommended them for a series of commissions for decorative schemes while they were still his pupils. When Gustav was only 17, he was helping to design a pageant for the Emperor Franz Josef's silver wedding celebrations.

In 1883, Gustav and Ernst Klimt and Franz Matsch left the School of Applied Arts and set up their own studio, where they immediately started

Klimt's Vienna
(below) Throughout his life, Gustav Klimt remained quintessentially Viennese. He loved the city's way of life, with its coffee houses and meeting places such as the elegant Ringstrasse, shown here, which was popular with fashionable society for the daily stroll.

Laufberger's class
(above) Gustav and his brother Ernst studied art under Professor Ferdinand Laufberger at the Kunstgewerbeschule in Vienna. This photograph of 1880 shows Gustav in the centre of the front row, with Ernst to the right and the distinguished. Laufberger to the left.

M. Lenz, Sirk-Ecke/Historisches Museum der Stadt Wien, Vienna

Major commission

(right) The most important commission of Klimt's early career was the staircase decoration of the Kunsthistorisches *Museum, carried out with his brother and Matsch. Klimt assimilated a wide range of styles to personify figures from the history of art. The beautiful and enigmatic figure in the centre represents the art of ancient Greece, with the black-figured Attic vase behind her.*

Kunsthistorisches Museum, Vienna

Burgtheater decorations

(below) In 1886, the Klimt brothers and Franz Matsch received a prestigious commission to paint the ceiling areas of two staircases in Vienna's Burgtheater. *Gustav introduced many antique motifs and artefacts into the decorations.*

work on a series of decorative projects for villas in Vienna and the provinces. Recognition for their work came quickly, and in 1886 the three young artists were given the prestigious task of decorating the ceiling and side staircases of Vienna's newly-built *Burgtheater*. The theme chosen for the decorations was the history of the theatre, and for his part Gustav depicted a number of historical scenes and classical allegories, as well as a curtain for the Auditorium. The success of the venture (which earned Klimt a Golden Cross of Merit) led to the most important commission of his

youth – completing the staircase decoration for Vienna's new *Kunsthistorisches* Museum.

The decorative scheme had been started by Vienna's foremost historical painter Hans Makart, but was left unfinished by his untimely death in 1884. Klimt and his colleagues had always admired the exuberance and flourish of Makart's work, so they were delighted to take over where he had left off. It fell to Gustav to fill many of the spaces left between pilasters with single figures representing the history of art from Ancient Egypt to the Renaissance. He approached the task with scholarly zeal, burying himself in art books and browsing in museums to collect ideas about the art of each period. The result was a series of quite remarkable portraits in different styles, varying from the rather two-dimensional portrayal of the Egyptian girl to the startlingly modern-looking girl from Ancient Greece (this page).

AN INDEPENDENT SPIRIT

By the time he was 35, Klimt had a reasonable body of work behind him and a growing reputation as a worthy successor to Hans Makart. To all outward appearances he was on his way to becoming a pillar of the Viennese art establishment. But privately he was not as much of a conformist as he may have seemed. Klimt was always a passionate champion of individual and artistic freedom, and something of a bohemian who was more at home wandering around in a voluminous blue 'monk's' smock than the suit adopted by many successful painters of his generation.

At around this time, the painter was getting to

Georg Riha

77

know a number of progressive artists and intellectuals who congregated in Vienna's many coffee houses, and he was also discovering European Impressionist and Symbolist painters through exhibitions of their work that were held in the city. Widening horizons fostered Klimt's discontent with the conservative attitudes of the Viennese Artists' Association (the *Künstlerhaus*) of which he was now a member, and in 1897 he and a group of friends resigned to set up their own organization. The group – which came to be known as the Secession – stood for a new attitude towards art, and sought to combat Vienna's inward-looking provincialism through an increased awareness of what was happening in the rest of Europe. Klimt, who was a man of few words, may seem in retrospect an unlikely leader of such a movement, but he was elected President of the Secession and threw himself into organizing its first exhibition with enormous enthusiasm.

At the time when the Secession was founded, Klimt still had one important commission left on his hands. In 1894, the Ministry of Education had approached him and Franz Matsch (Ernst Klimt had died in 1892) to ask if they would produce a series of designs for the ceiling of the Great Hall at Vienna University. After a great deal of debate, it was settled that Klimt should tackle three panels on the themes of 'Philosophy', 'Medicine' and 'Jurisprudence', which represented three of the University's faculties. It was a mammoth undertaking, and something of an artistic and physical challenge for Klimt. A friend who visited him in his studio while he was at work on *Philosophy* left this impression of the artist's creative struggle: 'It was afternoon, 35 degrees centigrade. He had on only his usual dark smock and nothing underneath. His life is spent in front of the great canvas, climbing up and down the ladder, pacing up and down, looking, brooding, creating out of nothing, trying, daring. He seems as if surrounded by a mist, wrestling with this element of uncertainty, kneading it, with both arms immersed up to the shoulders . . .'

Klimt's efforts did not produce their desired effects. The University professors, who had naturally assumed that the panels would resemble his previous work, were rather horrified to see

The 'Klimt Affair'

In 1894, Franz Matsch and Gustav Klimt were commissioned to produce a series of paintings for the ceiling of the Great Hall at Vienna University. When Klimt exhibited his first picture, *Philosophy*, at the Secession in 1900, the critics accused him of having produced a painting that was chaotic, nonsensical, and out of keeping with its intended setting as well as out of style with Matsch's work. *Medicine* and *Jurisprudence* were also greeted with abuse, and although the Ministry of Education approved the ceiling paintings in 1903, Klimt was so offended by the outcry that he abandoned the scheme in 1905.

Galerie Welz, Salzburg

Medicine
(left and detail right) Klimt's controversial panels for the University could have been among his most outstanding achievements had they not been destroyed by fire in 1945. Most highly acclaimed was Medicine, *which now only survives as a photograph. Two-thirds of the picture is taken up with a 'column of humanity'; the only surviving colour photograph (right) gives an idea of the rich textures and colours he employed.*

Galerie Welz, Salzburg

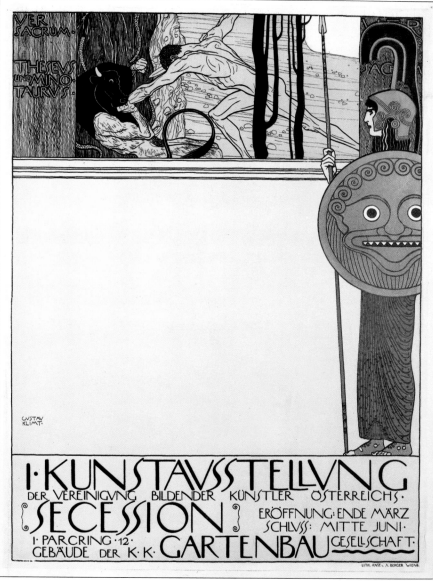

Klimt's popularity as a painter of female portraits was probably due in part to his ability to flatter women and produce images of languid elegance. It also fitted into his overwhelming fascination with the female sex. The artist had a roving eye for beautiful women, and he once even pursued the famous Viennese beauty Alma Mahler to Venice where he begged her with impassioned pleas to become his lover – a desire that remained unfulfilled. Klimt never married, but he did enjoy a 27-year liaison with his sister-in-law Emilie Flöge, who owned a fashion shop in Vienna. Even though the couple did not choose to formalize their union, Klimt was genuinely devoted to Emilie and he spent almost every

Secessionist poster
(left) Disillusioned with the reactionary policies of the official Viennese Society of Artists, Klimt and others formed their own exhibiting body – the Secession.

Emilie Flöge
(below) Klimt had a close relationship with Emilie Flöge, who ran a fashion shop in Vienna. He would design exotic dresses for the shop and she, in turn, would model for him.

Philosophy represented as a nebulous spiral of naked humanity ascending to a starry firmament accompanied by a huge misty female face. The other two panels, *Medicine* and *Jurisprudence*, completed in following years, only added fuel to the growing controversy, and the daily press began to publish hostile reviews accusing Klimt of pornography and trying to pervert Viennese youth. At first, the artist tried to work on and complete the project despite the fuss, but by 1905 he was so disillusioned that he abandoned the scheme, denouncing censorship and proclaiming himself for artistic freedom. What mattered to him now was personal satisfaction.

In the event, the scandal of the University paintings did not have a devastating effect upon Klimt's career. Although he no longer received official commissions from the City Council, there were plenty of private patrons who were interested in his work. He was now being sought out as a portraitist, particularly by the artistically inclined wives of Viennese industrialists, and he was able to carry out some of his most daring pictorial experiments in his pictures of well-to-do Viennese ladies.

Self-Portrait as Genitalia
(below) Klimt was renowned for his voracious sexual appetite and relentless pursuit of beautiful women. Making reference to this, he depicted himself in this very frank caricature.

Georg Riha

The Upper Belvedere
(above) Although Klimt's work shocked his Viennese contemporaries, today it hangs in Vienna's museums and the Belvedere has the largest collection.

summer for 20 years with her and her family at fashionable lakeside resorts at Attersee, where he was able to indulge his love of swimming, rowing and motor boats. It was here, too, that Klimt first turned his artistic abilities to landscape painting.

During the winter months in Vienna, Klimt's life fell into an unvarying routine. The artist would rise early, stroll over to the Café Tivoli for breakfast, and then return to his studio for an uninterrupted day's toil, only stopping work on his easel painting to make the occasional drawing from one of the many life models who were always in the studio. In the late evening, he would return to the café and relax in the company of friends, among whom he was known as 'king' because he

Stoclet Frieze
(left) Klimt's Stoclet Frieze was one of his most grandiose schemes and was heavily influenced by the mosaics he had seen in Ravenna. He combined these Byzantine sources with those of Japanese, Egyptian and Mycenaean art. Deeply concerned with textures, Klimt's materials included gold, silver, coral and semi-precious stones set into a background of white marble. The overall emphasis is on the exotic, as is shown in this working drawing for the Tree of Life.

Galerie Welz, Salzburg

Österreichisches Museum fur angewandte Kunst, Vienna

Model for the Stoclet Palace
(right) Given absolute artistic freedom, Josef Hoffmann created a building of harmonious proportions and perfect unity. The exterior was matched by an equally elegant interior.

was generally considered to be the best painter of them all.

NEW TALENTS

Klimt and his circle of friends formed a very close group. They left the Secession in 1905 after the 18th group exhibition, and began to show their work on their own. Their exhibiting body sought to foster the newest talent in Vienna, and Klimt soon found himself acting as mentor to a younger generation of painters. Egon Schiele, some 28 years' Klimt's junior, began showing with the new group as early as 1909, when he was just 19. His first paintings betrayed an enormous debt to Klimt, whose work he admired greatly. The admiration was not one-sided either: the two men exchanged drawings and Klimt also introduced his young protegé to new patrons. He was also zealous on Oscar Kokoschka's behalf, and strongly defended the decision to include Kokoschka's work in the group exhibitions, despite the fact that it was publicly disliked, on the grounds that Kokoschka was an outstandingly talented painter.

The rift between the Klimt circle and the other

Egon Schiele
(left) Klimt and Schiele met at the Vienna Academy of Fine Arts in 1907. The two became close friends and greatly admired one another's work, and for a time, both influenced each other. Schiele's work was exhibited with the group formed by ex-members of the Secession, known as the Kunstschau, of which Klimt was also a member. Schiele soon developed his own, highly personal style, which is characterized by an intense, almost tortured, expressiveness.

The Stoclet Palace

When the Belgian millionaire Adolphe Stoclet commissioned Josef Hoffmann to design a villa in Brussels for him in 1904, he allowed the architect complete freedom to indulge his imagination and an unlimited budget. The building was intended as a complete work of art, and the Wiener Werkstätte collaborated with Hoffmann on all the interior decorations. Klimt was given his only opportunity to experiment with real mosaic when he was asked to design a frieze for the dining-room. The frieze runs the whole length of the room above the level of the sideboard. The two long walls are both decorated with the curling branches of the Tree of Life; on one wall the figure of a young woman symbolizes Expectation, while on the opposite side an embracing couple symbolizes Fulfilment.

Georg Riha

Secessionist artists had really occurred because one group favoured 'pure painting' while Klimt and his friends – who included architects and designers as well as artists – sought to bridge the gap between painting and the applied arts. Indeed, the greatest achievement of Klimt's mature years – the decoration of the Stoclet Palace in Brussels begun in 1909 – involved the successful collaboration of the artist and the *Wiener Werkstätte*, a craft workshop that had been set up to produce high quality objects, fabrics and furniture in the Secessionist style. The project came about when the Belgian millionaire Adolphe Stoclet asked the architect Josef Hoffmann to design a villa for him in Brussels. No expense was to be spared, and all the decorations and accessories, down to the wine glasses and cutlery, were to be designed in harmony with the whole. Klimt's contribution to the vast project was his frieze for the dining room, which was inlaid with gold, mosaic and precious stones, and which showed *Expectation* along one wall and *Fulfilment* (pp.84-5) facing it. This complete work of art in one building was to be the last great flowering of Viennese Art Nouveau.

Once the Stoclet Palace frieze was finished,

Klimt turned his attentions back to easel painting, and to landscape and portraiture in particular. He became more isolated and set in his ways than before, leaving Vienna only once or twice a year to take the waters at Bad Gastein, or to visit his friends the Primavesis, who held an annual barbecue for Klimt's circle in Moravia.

On the morning of 11 January 1918, as Klimt was dressing for his breakfast stroll to the Café Tivoli, he suddenly experienced a massive stroke. He was rushed to hospital and kept alive for three weeks, but pneumonia set in, and he died on 6 February. Klimt left many unfinished works in his studio, but thieves broke in while he was in hospital and stole several of the canvases. One of those that they left was *The Bride* (p.83), whose overtly erotic nature they may perhaps have found too shocking. Yet the painting was a perfect reflection of the libidinous preoccupations of Klimt's Vienna, and it expressed, in its handling of the subject, the essence of his art.

The painter's garb
(below) This photograph of Klimt, taken a few years before his death, shows him outside his much-loved studio in Josefstädterstrasse, clad in the full-length blue smock in which he always worked and would greet all his visitors. Although Klimt was often uncommunicative, Schiele said of his friend: 'Klimt's generosity of spirit was genuine; he was not a hermit, and was even very welcoming, though he knew well who his real friends were.'

Historisches Museum der Stadt Wien, Vienna

Erotic Opulence

The decorative beauty of Klimt's paintings, which shimmer with the intensity of pure gold studded with jewels, apparently masks but actually enhances the eroticism of his work.

Klimt's lifetime spanned the most exciting epoch in Viennese cultural history. The artist was born only six years after Sigmund Freud, and the Viennese writers and thinkers of his generation were those who produced the theories of psychoanalysis, sexuality and aesthetics that were to challenge established notions of behaviour and to form the basis of modern thought. Beneath the city's conservative facade ran a newly-discovered fascination with the human psyche and with sex in particular. The central thematic obsessions of Klimt's art – eroticism, cycles of life, generation and death, and female power and sexuality – mirror quite accurately the concerns of intellectuals in Vienna at the turn of the century, and show the artist to have been entirely in tune with his times.

From the start of his artistic career, Klimt demonstrated an overwhelming preoccupation with the image of woman, and, like many Symbolist painters of his time, he displayed a curious ambiguity of attitude towards the female sex. The women in Klimt's pictures are both Madonnas and 'femmes fatales'. The artist's

The Black Feather Hat
(right) Klimt occasionally abandoned his taste for elaborate gold ornament in favour of a simpler, more Impressionistic, style. He was fascinated by the high-fashion hats and gorgeous clothes of Vienna's real-life femmes fatales.

Birch Wood
(below) In addition to portraits, Klimt painted a number of decorative landscapes in a glittering pointillist style. His few forest scenes show an obvious delight in the repetition of verticals formed by the slender tree-trunks.

Claus Hansmann/Artothek

frequent use of the frontal pose often makes them seem like remote icons to be venerated or, conversely, like terrifying incarnations of evil. Klimt's women possess the power to lure men to destruction, like *Judith I* (p.90), or to provide happiness and liberation as in *The Kiss* (p.99). As his art developed, Klimt extended his depiction of women to include their entire life cycle, producing several pictures of maidens, pregnant women and mothers, often juxtaposed with decaying bodies or new images suggestive of death.

Klimt seems to have wanted to convey through his paintings the cyclical nature of human experience and the inevitability of joy and suffering. The way in which he communicated his ideas was not by manipulating the faces and bodies of his subjects into expressions of anguish, like Schiele and Kokoschka, but through his highly

Neue Galerie der Stadt Linz

Österreichische Galerie, Vienna

schematized compositions and use of symbolic detail. Klimt was a fine draughtsman who possessed an outstanding ability to delineate the human body in a few elegant lines, but in his paintings he chose to subordinate human beings to the decorative richness of the surface. The eye of the spectator is constantly drawn to ornamental details that can be read as eyes, spirals, cellular forms, tendrils, spermatozoa, and ova, and which enhance the meaning of the paintings through their suggestive qualities. In contrast to these shimmering layers of ornament, the faces in the pictures seem strangely impassive, and the figures quite static. It is as though they are embedded or imprisoned in the decor to which they are a mere accessory. There is also an odd interplay between Klimt's highly naturalistic, almost photographic, manner of portraying faces and the artificial environment in which he places them, that gives his work its particular distinction.

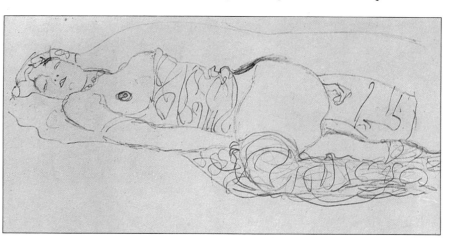

Erotic masterpieces
(left) Klimt was a marvellous draughtsman, evoking the sensuality of the female form in a few vigorous strokes of grey pencil on very fine rice-paper. His beautiful drawings are nearly always erotic, concentrating on the body's anticipation of sexual fulfilment or the relaxed abandonment of sexual gratification.

Private Collection, Graz

The Bride (unfinished)
(right) This painting, which was found in Klimt's studio at his death, gives us an unusual insight into his working methods and character. The bride's head has been sketchily wrapped, at the throat, in a transparent drapery which creates a morbid effect of decapitation. The rest of the body, depicted in intimate detail, was in the process of being decoratively obscured.

Galerie Welz, Salzburg

Private Collection

Joachim Blauel/Artothek

Fulfilment
(right and detail above) In this famous cartoon for the Stoclet Frieze *(p.81), Klimt depicts the sensual experience of fulfilment. The decorative overlay is used to symbolize the union of the two lovers. Their embracing forms are completely engulfed in a dazzling ornamental mosaic of organic and biological forms. In among the spirals and squares are exotic phallus-shaped birds, fish and eye motifs. The spiralling branches behind them stem from the* Tree of Life *(p.80) – an age-old symbol of fertility.*

Of course, the highly decorative nature of many of Klimt's pictures relates to his training as a decorative artist, and to the fact that many of the paintings were designed to be seen as part of an entire ornamental scheme in an interior. But the approach also spilled over into the easel paintings and portraits, where the frames are often an integral part of the pictures and as important as the canvases, themselves. No doubt Klimt had at the back of his mind the craftsmanship of his goldsmith father, and the insistence of the Arts and Crafts movement that there should be no distinction between decorated objects and paintings. The costly materials that he sometimes used in his works also serve to illustrate the artist's perception of his paintings as precious objects in themselves.

EROTIC SOURCES

The originality of Klimt's style arose from the fact that he was highly eclectic in approach and drew upon many different sources of visual imagery. He began by emulating the exuberant Baroque style of Hans Makart, moved on to a manner of almost Pre-Raphaelite clarity, and then went back in time to look closely at the art of Ancient Egypt and Greece. In several pictures – the *Expectation* cartoon for example – stiff poses, shallow pictorial space and a severe, almost geometric stylization of figures, show his debt to art of that period. The Byzantine mosaics that Klimt saw on a trip to Ravenna were also very important for his art, and the parallel between their gold-encrusted surfaces and his own paintings is obvious. Later in life, Klimt's collection of Japanese prints and vases became a new source of ideas. Some of the late portraits show fashionable Viennese ladies set against

COMPARISONS

Byzantine Mosaics

The art of mosaic, in which small fragments of glass or marble are set in plaster to create pictures and patterns, originated in classical times and became increasingly popular with the rise of Christianity. Mosaics are often a prominent feature of Byzantine churches, and Klimt saw some of the most outstanding examples on his trip to Ravenna in 1903. Because he had been trained in mosaic technique, he was able to translate the glittering, richly-encrusted surfaces of these works into his paintings. The stiff, frontally presented figures and shallow space of the Ravenna mosaic of San Vitale and the abstract spirals of the Tree of Life in the apse of San Clemente in Rome are all echoed in Klimt's work. Contemporaries immediately recognized the 'Byzantine' quality of his pictures, even with the intrusion of Egyptian, Japanese and Mycenaean elements.

S. Vitale, Ravenna

The Empress Theodora San Vitale, Ravenna
(above) The spectacular mosaics of the Empress Theodora and the Emperor Justinian (not shown) flank a glowing vision of Christ with saints. As in Klimt's paintings, the heads are real portraits, while the draperies are highly stylized and decorative.

S. Clemente, Rome

The Tree of Life San Clemente, Rome
(left) This very fine mosaic, with its delicate, spiralling forms, is reflected in Klimt's own Tree of Life (p.80).

Musée des Beaux-Arts, Strasbourg

backgrounds of Japanese warriors and geishas that were copied from the objects in his studio.

Klimt was familiar with works by the Impressionists, and the gauzy effects of some of his portraits prompts comparison with Monet or Whistler. His early essays in landscape also show an Impressionistic interest in the transient gleam of light upon water, but the majority of the landscapes are not concerned with the pursuit of natural appearances. Generally speaking, there is no sense of space or air in Klimt's hermetically sealed universe. The artist observed nature as though he was looking through a tiny grid, preferring to focus on small details rather than vast panoramic vistas. The horizon line is often very high or completely absent, so the sky does not intrude, and nature becomes an artificial mosaic assembled from various brightly-coloured gems dotted carefully across the canvas.

This process of abstracting pattern from nature and recording shapes and colours for their pleasing visual qualities or symbolic associations, rather than attempting to portray the world in a naturalistic manner is what makes Klimt a modern artist. It forms a link between his work and that of painters like Wassily Kandinsky and Paul Klee who were to take the development of abstraction one step further.

Judith I

In the Old Testament, the Jewish widow Judith saved the city of Bethulia from siege by the Assyrians by adorning herself and venturing into the enemy camp to gain access to the Assyrian general, Holofernes. He invited her to a banquet intending to seduce her, and while they were alone after the feast, Judith took advantage of Holofernes' drunkenness to decapitate him, and returned to Bethulia with his head in a sack. The Jews saw Judith as a virtuous heroine, but Klimt portrays her as a Viennese femme fatale. Her expression of cruel triumph has often led to her being confused with Salome, who ordered the beheading of John the Baptist to satisfy the vengeful spirit of her mother.

Judith II
(right) Klimt returned to the Judith theme in 1909, with his life-size portrait of Judith II. *The gaunt figure is even more chilling and predatory than* Judith I, *clutching the hair of the decapitated Holofernes in her fleshless fingers.*

Assyrian landscape
(below) The stunning gold background, with its schematized fig trees and grapevines, is taken from a famous Assyrian relief (right).

Österreichische Galerie, Vienna

Ca' Rezzonico, Venice

Fotostudio Otto

Scala

Salome
(above) Many of Klimt's contemporaries refused to believe that his triumphant femme fatale represented the pious heroine Judith. During his lifetime it was listed as a 'Salome' – the deadly temptress favoured by the other fin-de-siècle figures, like Aubrey Beardsley.

Biblical site
(below) Klimt's quote from the Assyrian palace relief of Sennacherib at Nineveh (705-681 BC) gives his Judith a precise biblical setting. Klimt enjoyed referring to esoteric sources, but did not always use them in an archaeological fashion.

Michael Holford

British Museum, London

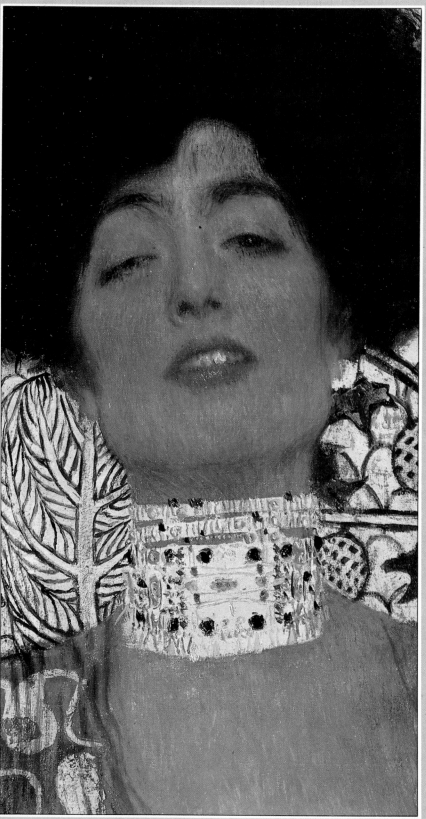

Death and Sexuality
(above) Judith's rapturous expression, and the jewelled choker which visually suggests decapitation, links her sexual ecstasy with the spectre of death.

Gallery

Klimt's art is dominated by images of women. He was extremely responsive to female beauty and could easily have made a prosperous living painting society ladies, as his portraits of Emilie Flöge and Margaret Stonborough-Wittgenstein demonstrate. However, most of his pictures take a more original and less straightforward view of women, stressing their sexual allure and mysterious qualities.

Klimt's work was attacked at the time as 'erotic pollution', but a later audience can see it as a subtle exploration of the ambivalent feelings that sex so often evokes. Judith, for example, is irresistibly seductive, but also repugnant because of the frisson of pleasure she seems to experience from the severed head of her victim. And the beguiling women in Water Serpents and Goldfishes have the air of enchantresses who lure men to their doom.

The appeal of Klimt's pictures, however, depends not only on his powerful, neurotic and often morbid sexuality, but also on his marvellous decorative skills. He was a master of linear rhythms, as the Beethoven Frieze demonstrates, and unrivalled in his ability to create stunningly sumptuous patterns, as in The Kiss.

Music I *1895*
14½″ × 17½″ Bayerischestaatsgemäldesammlungen,
Neue Pinakothek, Munich

Klimt made at least two other versions of this subject – another painting and a coloured lithograph. This early treatment is a good example of the kind of romantic and symbolic subject that was all the rage in the German-speaking world of this period, and the frieze-like composition also shows Klimt's traditionalism early in his career. His originality, however, comes out in the use of flat areas of gold. The picture is replete with symbolic allusions – the sphinx, for example, represents poetic fantasy – and conveys a feeling of romantic languor.

Fotostudio Otto

Judith I *1901*
33″ × 16½″ Österreichische
Galerie, Vienna

The aggressive decadence of this painting soon won it notoriety, and even though the subject is clearly stated on the frame, the picture was often called Salome. (Judith was a Jewish heroine who decapitated an enemy general, but Salome was the temptress who caused St John the Baptist to be executed). It is indeed one of the archetypal images of the femme fatale, Judith's parted lips and half-closed eyes giving her an intensely erotic look. Her hand rests almost caressingly on Holofernes' severed head, and her bizarre costume enhances the mood of morbid sensuality.

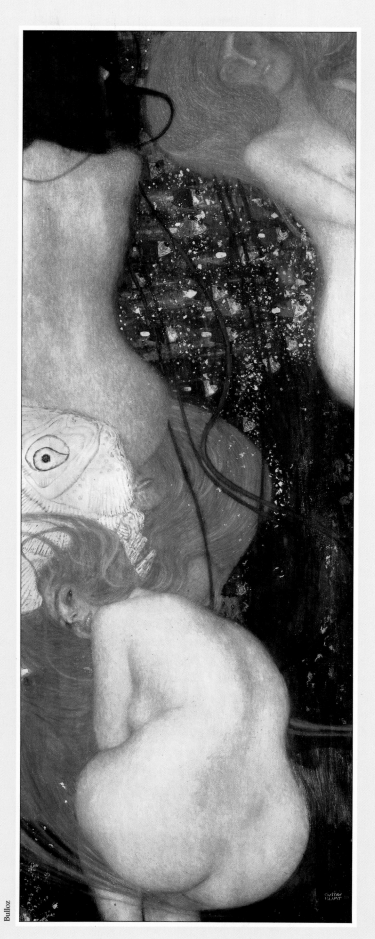

Bulloz

Goldfish *1901-02*
71¼″ × 26¼″ Private Collection

Klimt originally wanted to call this picture 'To my Critics', intending it as a riposte to those who had attacked his ceiling painting for the University of Vienna; the figure at the base who turns towards the spectator with a look of blatant sexual invitation is very similar to one in Medicine *(p.78) that he eventually painted over. When the picture was shown at Düsseldorf in 1902, it was attacked by the critics and, as one contemporary recalled, it was 'requested that the Ministry of Education remove the painting before the beginning of the exhibition, for the German Crown Prince who was to open it might be shocked'.*

The Beethoven Frieze, detail: The Hostile Powers 1902
33" high Österreichische Galerie, Vienna

The Beethoven frieze was painted to accompany the exhibition of a statue of Beethoven by Max Klinger. In this section Klimt depicted the powers 'hostile' to Happiness: The giant Typhon (the ape); his daughters, the three Gorgons; Sickness, Mania, Death (behind); Desire and Impurity, Excess.'

92

The Beethoven Frieze, detail: Pure Joy 1902
33" high Österreichische Galerie, Vienna

When the frieze was first exhibited, the accompanying catalogue provided the following description: 'The Longing for Happiness finds solace in Poetry. The arts lead us into the ideal realm in which we find pure joy, pure happiness, pure love. Choir of the angels of Paradise.'

Emilie Flöge *1902*
71¼″ × 33″ Historisches
Museum der Stadt,
Vienna

*Emilie Flöge was Klimt's
mistress and the owner of
a haute couture salon in
Vienna for which Klimt
designed several dresses.
This majestic but tender
image of her is a key work
in the development of
Klimt's portraiture,
marking his move away
from a comparatively
naturalistic Impressionist
style to his own highly
original manner of
combining realism with
flattened patterns.*

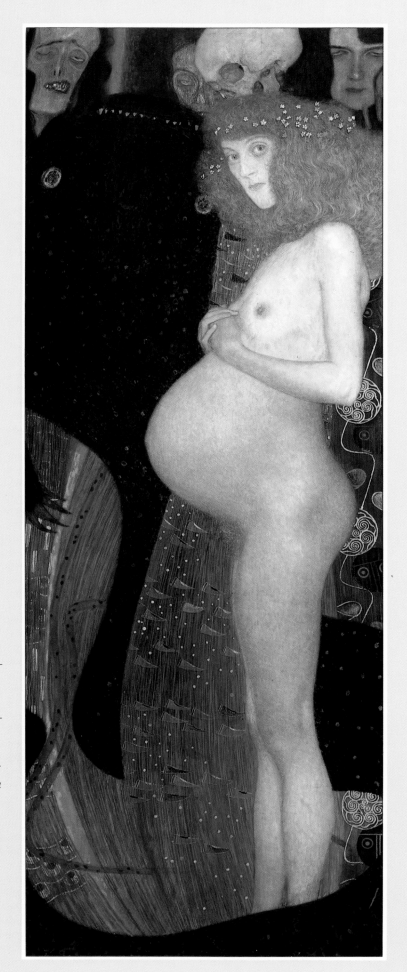

Hope I *1903*
71¼″ × 26½″ National Gallery of
Canada, Ottawa

*Fritz Wärndorfer, the patron who
originally owned this painting, kept
it in a specially constructed shrine
behind locked doors, an indication of
the strange air of sanctity with which
Klimt has imbued this startling
image. The pregnant woman stares
quizzically at the spectator, while
behind her are sinister, threatening
figures, suggesting all the perils the
unborn child will have to face. Her
voluptuously curved belly contrasts
with her spindly limbs, conveying a
sense of the fragility of life. Klimt
painted another picture of Hope in
1907-08, this time showing the
mother-figure clothed.*

Fotostudio Otto

**Water Serpents II
(Women Friends)** *c.1904-07*
19¾" × 7¾" Österreichische
Galerie, Vienna

*This small and densely
ornamented painting shows
Klimt's technique at its most
exquisite. There is almost no
sense of three-dimensionality in
the slender forms of the two
figures, which are swept up in
the sinuous, rhythmic flow of
pattern. Klimt experimented
boldly with materials, and here —
as in many of his works — he has
made lavish use of gold.*

Margaret Stonborough-Wittgenstein *1905*
70¾″ × 35½″ Bayerische-staatsgemälde-sammlungen, Neue Pinakothek, Munich

Klimt's female portraits are usually very simple and striking in composition – he places the figure centrally on the canvas and sets off the delicately observed flesh areas against bold, flat areas of pattern in the background. Here the pose is particularly splendid, the graceful curves of the shoulders and neck being beautifully depicted.

Artothek

Galerie Welz, Salzburg

Danaë *c.1907-08*
32¼″ × 32¾″ Private Collection

*Towards the end of his career, Klimt made several pictures of
mythological subjects, of which Danaë, who was ravished by Jupiter in
the form of a shower of gold, is the most openly erotic. The critic Eduard
Pötzl wrote an attack on the picture: 'This Danaë is rolled up like a
bundle of old washing, and in this position, which no woman in the
world has ever assumed of her own free will, she permits us to admire
her thigh and half her bosom.'*

Fotostudio Otto

The Kiss *c.1907-08*
70¾″ × 70¾″ Österreichische Galerie, Vienna

*This is one of the culminating works of Klimt's career and for once it
was officially acclaimed from the beginning, being bought for the
Austrian government when it was first exhibited. It takes to the
ultimate extreme Klimt's love of decorative splendour, with the
beautiful patterning of flowers and the heads and hands of the lovers
emerging from a dazzling patchwork of gold and glittering ornament.
It is also his most powerful statement on the theme of the embrace.*

IN THE BACKGROUND

The Secession

R. Volkel; Café Griensteidl/Historisches Museum der Stadt Wien, Vienna

The Secessionists broke away from the stifling academicism of the Austrian art establishment, bringing Viennese culture into the 20th century, and were greeted with tremendous enthusiasm.

Bildarchiv der Österreichischen Nationalbibliothek, Vienna

barriers between fine and applied art. At the Café Zum Blauen Freihaus, artists Josef Engelhart and Johann Krämer met, both of whom were strongly influenced by contemporary French art. With Alfred Roller, Ernst Stöhr and Adolf Böhm, they formed a coterie that was nicknamed the Hagenbund after the café's owner. Nearby, at the Café Sperl, the more exclusive 'Club of Seven' was formed, which included the brilliant graphic artist, Kolomon Moser and protégés of Vienna's most celebrated modern architect, Otto Wagner. Common to these, and other artistic coteries, was a new aestheticism – a need to free art from its commercial limitations, and make the quest for

The Secessionists
(left) This photograph was taken at the Secessionists' 14th exhibition, dedicated to Beethoven, in 1902. Klimt wears an artist's smock: Koloman Moser is in front of him.

The Mahdi's Tomb
(below and right) Josef Olbrich designed both the exhibition hall (nicknamed the Mahdi's tomb) and the poster for the Secessionists' second exhibition in 1898.

'The future is blooming all around us; but we are still rooted in the past', lamented the Viennese writer, Hermann Bahr, in 1891. It was a sentiment shared by many of the artists who congregated in Vienna at this time. While the public life of the city remained staunchly conservative, a new avant-garde emerged whose aim was to broaden the narrow 19th-century approaches to painting, architecture and design. If they had no common philosophy behind them, they were united in their desire to find an alternative to the reactionary *Künstlerhaus* (the Society of Artists), who owned the city's only exhibition hall. And it was from this desire that the Secession was born, propelling Viennese art into the modern world.

The ideas behind the Secession were first born in the coffee-houses of Vienna, which provided an environment quite different to the stifling academicism of the Künstlerhaus. Here artists, writers, musicians and philosophers could meet freely, discuss alternatives to the staid conventions of naturalism, or ways of replacing the traditional

H. Zdrazil

Café Griensteidl
(above) As the end of the century approached, the Viennese looked forward to a new age and this was excitedly debated in coffee houses, like the Café Griensteidl. These were the meeting-places of politicians, artists and literati, and each person knew who was to be found at which coffee house and at what hour.

Georg Riha

The father of modern Viennese architecture
(above) Otto Wagner's revolutionary buildings allied him to the Secessionists. His decorative ceramic façade of the apartment block, the Majolika Haus, was a departure from the traditional sculptural devices.

Graphische Sammlung Albertina, Vienna

beauty its own justification.

Inevitably, these ideas led to a conflict with the Künstlerhaus, and this was brought to a head in 1896, when the arch-reactionary Eugen Felix was re-elected as the organization's president. Felix had taken a personal hand in preventing the work of Vienna's Impressionists from being shown in Künstlerhaus exhibitions, and in excluding young artists' work from any shows of Austrian painting that were sent abroad. His appointment was the cue for the coffee-house rebels to stand up in 1897 and form the Secession – a new, independent exhibiting society. The majority of the 40 founder-members of the Secession were also members of the Künstlerhaus and, at first, they hoped to remain as members of both bodies. But the Künstlerhaus reacted angrily to their move, forcing them to resign within two months.

AIMS OF THE SECESSION

The Secessionists had two basic aims: to introduce the Viennese public to new art, and bring the city's artists into contact with the latest international trends. These aims were to be achieved through their own exhibitions, at which foreign artists would be represented, and through their magazine, *Ver Sacrum* (Sacred Spring). The magazine's title came from an ancient Roman ritual of consecration whereby, in times of national danger, the elders pledged their children to a

divine mission to save society. But in the Vienna of 1897, it was the young who were pledging themselves to save culture from the hard-boiled elders of the Künstlerhaus, bringing together a host of modern influences – ranging from Impressionism to Art Nouveau – into a forum that would encourage change and experimentation.

Gustav Klimt, who had long been in revolt against the Künstlerhaus, was elected the Secession's first president. For the first Secession exhibition in 1898, he devised a poster of Theseus slaying the Minotaur to liberate the youth of Athens (p.79). Although the censor forced Klimt to cover his Theseus with a tree trunk for modesty, this and other Secession posters were to both shock and enthrall Vienna's hypersensitive public.

The architects Hoffmann and Olbrich were responsible for arranging the exhibits at this first Secession show, and their innovative approach meant that paintings were hung at eye-level against plain backgrounds, and that works by the same artist were grouped together. In addition to the contributions of the Secessionists themselves, works by Rodin, Segantini, Whistler, Walter Crane, and the much admired Belgian painter

Georg Riha

second exhibition in 1898. Olbrich wanted to create a 'quiet and elegant' place where modern man could escape from the pressures of city life. Most traditional galleries and museums have been modelled on Renaissance palaces, but Olbrich chose the pagan temple as his model. Inside there was plenty of light and space, with the use of movable partitions for the first time. Outside, the building's most striking feature was its open-work dome of gilded laurel leaves. Across the Secession temple's portals was the defiant motto: 'To the Age its Art, to Art its Freedom.'

Within a year of their revolt, the Secessionists

Fernand Khnopff, were exhibited. Most novel, however, was the Secession show's mixed character, comprising not only paintings but also graphics, sculpture, architectural designs and objects of applied art. 'Even if you do not like pictures,' the first issue of *Ver Sacrum* proclaimed, 'let us decorate your walls with beautiful hangings; would you not care to drink your wine out of an artistically fashioned glass? Come to us, we will show you the design for a vessel worthy of the noble wine.' Following this example, the Fifth Secession exhibition, in 1899, was devoted exclusively to drawings and graphics, and the Eighth, in 1900, at which the work of Charles Rennie Mackintosh was prominent, was taken up primarily with applied art and design.

THE FIRST EXHIBITION

In Vienna, some 57,000 people responded to the Secessionists' invitation to modern art, and the first exhibition was a tremendous commercial and critical success. 'Herr Felix, big business!' one critic gloated to the Künstlerhaus president, 'Just think! The Viennese – your Viennese, Herr Felix, whom you thought you knew so well – come by the dozen to buy works of art.' Armed with overnight acclaim, the Secessionists were able to think about a building of their own. With the help of sympathizers on the city council, including Mayor Karl Lüeger, and money from well-wishers such as Karl Wittgenstein (one of Klimt's patrons), a site near the chief street market was found.

Within six months, the building designed by Joseph Maria Olbrich had sprung up in time for a

Art and the railway
(above) The Secessionists' ideal of bringing the standards of fine art to everyday objects and buildings is exemplified by Otto Wagner and Joseph Maria Olbrich's work on the Vienna railway system. In all, 36 stations were required, and, as with the Karlsplatz stop, Wagner had control of the design of each one.

The work of Adolf Böhm
(right) The two designs of Böhm's shown here, the floral one being a book decoration and the other a design for silk embroidery, clearly illustrate why his designs, alongside those of Klimt, Kurzweil and Moser, put the Secessionist magazine, Ver Sacrum, *in the vanguard of spreading the new art.*

Graphische Sammlung Albertina, Vienna

and their unusual building, which was nicknamed the 'Golden Cabbage' by the stallholders in the nearby market, were an approved part of Vienna's culture. Although Klimt would never be welcomed into the Establishment fold, there were official commissions and professorships at the School of Applied Arts for other leading Secessionists. Their acceptance by the Viennese had been signalled by the visit to the first exhibition of the aged emperor of Austria himself. He was greeted by the esteemed water-colourist Rudolf von Alt, who had upset his former colleagues at the Künstlerhaus by agreeing to become the Secession's honorary president. The emperor must have been surprised to meet with the rebel artists in crisp white shirts and tails, but his presence at their exhibition illustrated conclusively that Vienna was now fixed on the map as a major centre of modern art.

Ornamental façades
(below) Early on, the decoration of buildings was important for Secessionist architecture, but under Otto Wagner, unity of construction took precedence.

Illustration for
Ver Sacrum
(right) Ver Sacrum *was the focal point for developments in graphic art. Illustrations like this by Koloman Moser showed the new trends.*

A Year in the Life 1914

The early months of 1914 were dominated by the Irish question in Britain, while across the Channel a newspaper office murder in Paris caused a sensation. In June, Archduke Ferdinand's assassination at Sarajevo sparked off the First World War which was to sweep away the Europe of Klimt and his contemporaries.

In 1914, the Irish question was once again a thorn in the side of British politics. The Liberal government had been trying to enact a Home Rule Bill since 1910, despite opposition from the House of Lords. The Lords' power of veto was subsequently quashed, but a third bill introduced in 1912 attracted opposition from Protestant Ulster. Led by Sir Edward Carson, Protestants organized and armed themselves to prevent the creation of an autonomous and Catholic Ireland in which they would be a minority. Conservative and military leaders openly connived at this, and in 1914, the 'Curragh Incident' showed that large numbers of officers were prepared to resign rather than use force against the north. However, the inevitable struggle was shelved when war broke out.

Militant Suffragette agitation was also in full swing. In

Recruitment propaganda
(right) This famous poster is one of the many that were issued by the British Parliamentary Recruiting Committee in the first months of the Great War. The Cabinet, who had hastily co-opted Lord Kitchener as Secretary of State for War, were against conscription and so he had to rely on voluntary recruitment. Patriotic fervour combined with public pressure created 500,000 volunteers for the first month of the war. Over the next year and a half, an average of more than 100,000 a month joined up, many of them destined for a muddy and inglorious death.

Private Collection

Daddy, what did YOU do in the Great War?

Bridgeman Art Library

Giancarlo Costa

Engineering triumph
(right) In 1904, the United States took over the Panama Canal zone after buying out the French shareholders and coming to an arrangement with the new Panamanian Republic. On 15 August, a decade later, the artificial high-level waterway with three massive lake and lock systems linking the Pacific and the Atlantic Ocean was opened to traffic.

March, a group of women made their protest by damaging Velázquez's celebrated painting *The Rokeby Venus* on public view at London's National Gallery. In Paris, an even more violent episode occurred in the offices of the newspaper *Le Figaro*. The editor, Gaston Calmette, had conducted a long and vitriolic campaign against the Finance Minister, Joseph Caillaux, which included publishing letters of a personal nature. Madame Caillaux, fearful of further revelations, went to see the editor with a Browning automatic hidden in her muff and shot him several times. A sympathetic jury acquitted the murderess on 28 July, the day Austria-Hungary declared war on Serbia. Three days later, a fanatical Nationalist youth shot the French Socialist leader, Jean Jaurès. By this time Germany and Russia were at war, France had begun to mobilize, and a general conflict which was to become one of the bloodiest in history was only a few days away.

ASSASSINATION AT SARAJEVO

The spark had been lit on 28 June by another assassination, that of the Austrian Archduke Franz Ferdinand and his wife at Sarajevo in Bosnia. The assassin, 18-year-old Gavrilo Princip, belonged to a terrorist organization sworn to liberate the Serbs of Bosnia from Austro-Hungarian rule. The Austrians suspected that the government of neighbouring Serbia had some foreknowledge of the murders, and demanded satisfaction. The Serbs called on the Russians for help and then the Germans and Turks were drawn in on the side of Austria-

Battle of the Marne
(left) On 2 September 1914, the German First Army under Kluck crossed the river Marne, only 50 miles from Paris. Battle commenced three days later when the French 6th Army unexpectedly ran into Kluck's flank. In six days, 57 Allied divisions fighting along a 125 mile front caused 53 German divisions to retreat to the Aisne and set up entrenchments.

'The U-Boats are out'
(below) This graphic German poster is a reminder of the powerful role that U-Boats were to play in the war, their numbers increasing from 28 in 1914 to a total of 371. In August 1914, a German submarine, U9, torpedoed three British cruisers in the North Sea. Two months later, a dreadnought sank after hitting a mine laid by a U-Boat.

Hungary against Russia, France and Britain.

Most people expected a short war involving just a few decisive battles, particularly Germany who was fighting on two fronts. Her leaders thus put into operation the Schlieffen Plan, devised a generation earlier: German armies would sweep through neutral Belgium, capture the Channel ports, and advance on Paris from the west; France would be knocked out in six weeks, leaving Germany free to deal with Russia.

The plan went wrong from the start, as Belgian resistance prevented the Germans from stopping the disembarkment of the British Expeditionary Force at the Channel ports. Nevertheless they drove hard for Paris, arriving within 20 miles of the capital, while the French government nervously withdrew to Bordeaux. The Germans' over-extended lines of supply, and the exceptionally hot summer subsequently took their toll. The French counter-attacked at the battle of the Marne driving the Germans back. They dug in along the River Aisne, and the Allies soon followed suit. The month-long first battle of Ypres established lines of trenches on each side which stretched right across northern France, where they were to remain in bloody deadlock for four terrible years.

On the eastern front the Russians proved capable of beating the Austrians but suffered two catastrophic defeats at the hands of the Germans – at Tannenberg and the Masurian Lakes. In the longer term, the British naval victory off the Falkland Islands, which destroyed the Germans' surface raiders, was more important: it meant that Britain could import what she needed while conducting an ultimately lethal blockade of her enemies.

Royal Geographical Society, London

Shackleton at Ocean Camp
(above) Sir Ernest Shackleton, veteran Antarctic explorer, set out as leader of the British Imperial Trans-Antarctic expedition in August 1914. He aimed to cross Antarctica via the South Pole. Tragically, the expedition ship Endurance was frozen in the Weddell Sea and eventually crushed by pack ice. Stores and equipment were transferred to an ice floe, dubbed Ocean Camp, which drifted west to Elephant Island. With a crew of five, Shackleton sailed to South Georgia for help, arriving in May 1916.

Feminist fury
(right) The eighteen months before the outbreak of war in 1914 were notable for the wildness of Suffragette tactics to secure votes for women. Emily Davidson threw herself under the King's horse at the 1913 Derby, railway stations were burnt, acid was poured in postboxes and hunger strikes continued. On 10 March 1914, suffragettes slashed Velázquez's Rokeby Venus on view in the National Gallery, London, as a protest against the centuries-old masculine conception of women's subservient role.

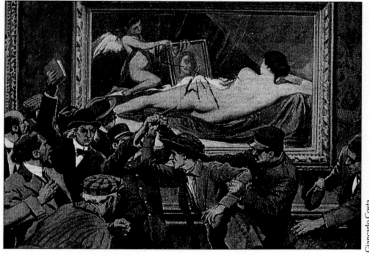

Giancarlo Costa

Edvard Munch: Self portrait/National Gallery, Oslo

EDVARD MUNCH

1863-1944

Edvard Munch was Norway's greatest painter and graphic artist, a major exponent of Symbolism and a forerunner of the Expressionists. The tragic loss of his mother and sister in his childhood brought a morbid tone to much of his work. Initially, his friendship with the bohemian circle in the Norwegian capital steered him towards Impressionism, but trips to Paris from 1889 onwards put him in touch with the Symbolists.

In 1892, Munch's name was made when his exhibition in Berlin was closed down, bringing him instant notoriety. Settling in Germany, he embarked on his *Frieze of Life,* a compilation of intensely personal images of love and death. Overwork, alcohol and emotional strain led Munch to a nervous breakdown in 1908. After this, he returned to live in seclusion in Norway, devoting his last years to public murals and studies of workers.

A Mind in Torment

Traumatic childhood experiences created in Munch a chronic anxiety and restlessness, leading ultimately to a nervous breakdown. After this, he returned to his native Norway to recuperate and settle.

Edvard Munch was born on 12 December 1863, in Løten, a small farming community in southern Norway. His father, Christian, came from a professional background of churchmen and soldiers and worked as a military physician. Christian's brother, Peter Andreas Munch, was a celebrated historian.

Edvard was the second son of five children. A year after his birth, the family moved to the capital, Christiania (re-named Oslo in 1927), where tragedy was to enter their lives. In 1868, Munch's mother died of tuberculosis at the age of 33 and, in 1877, his favourite sister Sophie also perished from the same disease. These early misfortunes scarred the boy deeply, and throughout his long career, images of the sick room and the deathbed recur constantly in his work.

Munch's home life was claustrophobic and oppressive. A sickly child himself, he was confined within the family flat for considerable periods of his youth, while his father's religious fervour, which had intensified after the death of his wife, was bringing him to the brink of insanity – for hours at a time, he would pace up and down his room in prayer. Small wonder that Munch later wrote of his childhood, 'Illness, madness and death were the black angels that kept watch over my cradle and accompanied me all my life.'

Fortunately, his aunt Karen had taken over the running of the family and was to prove a stabilizing influence. As an amateur painter, she encouraged the Munch children to draw. Accordingly, Edvard made copies of the illustrations in Grimm's fairy tales and, in the early 1880s, was trying to sell his work to magazines.

By this time, he had already decided on art as a career. His studies in engineering at the Technical College had lasted less than a year and, in 1881, he entered the State School of Art and Crafts. His initial supervisor there was Julius Middelthun, but

Munch Museum, Oslo

A family group
(above) Edvard is here shown (standing, right) with his mother, brother and sisters. His happy childhood was irreparably disrupted by the premature deaths of his mother and favourite sister, Sophie.

Norway's capital
(left) Christiania – modern Oslo – was a small provincial town when the Munch family moved there in 1864. Its deep-seated philistinism was slow to change, and explains the later vilification of Munch.

Archiv für Kunst und Geschichte

to see most of the latest works by Monet and the Impressionists.

Some Parisian influences can be detected in Munch's first masterpiece, *The Sick Child* (p.120), which was completed in 1886. However, the scraping away of the features and the slightly simplified forms created a more powerful emotional impact than most Impressionist paintings, and are reminiscent of Post-Impressionist masters like Vuillard and Ensor.

A SCHOLARSHIP TO PARIS

Four years later, Munch was able to study French art at greater leisure. After the success of his first one-man show, the Norwegian government awarded him a State Scholarship on condition that he found an acceptable teacher. Accordingly, on his arrival in Paris, he enrolled in the life classes of Léon Bonnat.

Munch worked diligently at these classes, but was soon alienated by his master's conventional academic approach. Bonnat, in turn, was impressed with his pupil's draughtsmanship, but objected to his highly subjective use of colour. The two men parted company after a disagreement over the precise tones of a wall in the studio.

Despite this setback, Munch's three-year stay in Paris was a crucial period. The death of his father in 1889 released him from lingering family ties while, on a more positive note, he benefited enormously from the feverish activity in the art world. He was particularly influenced by the

Family Evening (1884)
(above) Munch achieved an early maturity after his father allowed him to go to art school. Munch's family and friends are often the subjects for his paintings of this period.

Léon Bonnat's studio
(right) Munch's teacher in Paris was the academic Léon Bonnat. Munch found his approach quite alien, and instead turned for inspiration to the new Symbolist movement.

the dominant influence on his early development was the naturalist painter, Christian Krohg. In 1882, along with six other artists, Munch rented a studio where Krohg provided informal instruction.

Through Krohg, Munch also came into contact with the bohemian circle of writers and painters who were in the forefront of artistic rebellion in Norway. Led by Krohg and the novelist Hans Jaeger, the group denounced bourgeois morality and pressed for radical, sexual and artistic freedom. In literature, they worshipped Zola and, in painting, they advocated an unstinting brand of realism. One commentator summed them up as 'that half-debauched, poverty-stricken, Christiania gypsy camp'.

Norway, however, was too provincial a platform for Munch's talents. In 1883, he attended the open-air academy run by Gauguin's brother-in-law, Frits Thaulow, and through him gained a travel grant to Paris two years later. The visit lasted only three weeks, but gave him the opportunity

Christiania bohemia

Munch was introduced to Christiania's circle of progressive writers, the bohemians, by his teacher, Christian Krohg, who had written a Zolaesque novel, *Albertine*, which was an attack on official prostitution. The bohemians had all been inspired by the avant-garde movements in Paris and clashed violently with Norway's entrenched middle class. Their presiding intellect was Hans Jaeger, whose autobiographical novel had been condemned as obscene and was confiscated. The bohemians met to discuss such burning issues as anarchism, determinism, freedom for women and free love, and in practising what they preached were ostracized by the rest of society. Munch was naturally attracted by the bohemian ideals of intellectual and artistic freedom, but because of his retiring nature was always to a certain extent the odd man out.

Hans Jaeger
(below) In 1926 Munch wrote: '. . . my ideas developed under the influence of the bohemians or rather of Hans Jaeger'. Highly intellectual and a committed anarchist, Jaeger had shocked the Norwegian bourgeoisie with his 'pornographic' book, From the Christiania Bohemians, *for which he was sentenced to two months' imprisonment. He spent the evening before he was due to go to prison with Munch, who later painted this portrait of him.*

growing Symbolist movement, which inspired his symbolic use of colour, his simplification of form, and even his subject matter of the femme fatale.

Meanwhile, a dramatic incident brought Munch international attention. In 1892, the Verein Berliner Künstler (Union of Berlin Artists) invited him to join their exhibition. His paintings caused an uproar and, after a week, the committee ordered him to remove his 'daubs'. But some of the Verein's members objected and, headed by Max Liebermann, left to form the Berlin Secession.

Munch was delighted by the furore and swiftly made arrangements to exhibit the works in Dusseldorf and Cologne. An extensive tour of German and Scandinavian cities followed and, through these shows, Munch earned as much from his percentage of the entrance fees as he did from the sales of his paintings. Encouraged by this

The Berlin scandal
(below) Munch's one-man show, held in Berlin in 1892, earned him international notoriety. One respected art critic wrote that his paintings had 'absolutely nothing to do with art' and the exhibition was closed in a week.

National Gallery, Oslo

Bildarchiv Preussischer Kulturbesitz

sudden notoriety, Munch settled in Berlin and soon became attached to a new artistic coterie, which met at Zum Schwarzen Ferkel (the Black Piglet). Among its more vocal members were the playwright August Strindberg, and the Polish novelist Stanislaw Przybyszewski.

Amid the highly charged atmosphere of the group's meetings, Munch formulated plans for his *Frieze of Life.* Through this ambitious scheme, he intended to assemble a number of paintings on linked themes and display them together, in the hope that the ensemble would create a symphonic effect. The binding theme was to be 'the poetry of life, love and death', seen through the distorting mirror of Munch's personal experiences, and the series included many of his greatest paintings. *The Scream* (p.122), *The Dance of Life* (pp.124-5), *Madonna, The Vampire* and *Jealousy* (p.114) were among the works selected.

THE MEANING OF THE *FRIEZE*

At the core of the *Frieze* was Munch's view of female sexual power. He depicted this in three stages – as awakening innocence, voracious sexuality and as an image of death. In many cases, these three facets were combined in a single picture. The lithograph of *Madonna,* for example, suggested innocence through its title and the sketchy halo, and yet at the same time Munch chose to show the woman at the point of orgasm and described her expression as a 'corpse's smile'. Meanwhile, in the border, sperm wriggled like worms away from a sickly embryo.

Munch's own relations with women reflected these troubled images. Although tall and good looking, he was wary of the opposite sex: the loss of his mother and sister may have made him afraid of relationships with women – he often portrayed love and death together. The family history of

A summer refuge
(above) Munch spent his summers relaxing at the house he rented in Åsgårdstrand. The light and landscape there had a lasting effect on his art.

Stéphane Mallarmé
(below) The ideas of the Symbolist poets, like Mallarmé, who sought to reveal the workings of the inner mind, were of vital importance to Munch.

The Tulla Larsen Affair

Munch's involvement with Tulla Larsen was the most dramatic of his ill-starred relationships with women. He believed that marriage would inhibit his art and that his predisposition towards mental illness would, in fact, make it criminal for him to marry.

Tulla, however, hounded Munch relentlessly even to the extent of arranging a mock deathbed scene where she threatened to shoot herself. As Munch struggled to wrest the gun from her, it went off and severed the top half of one of his fingers. An ironical twist to the affair was that the injury subsequently made it painful for Munch to hold his palette.

Munch Museum, Oslo

Portrait of a lover
(above) Tulla Larsen was infatuated with Munch and they did actually discuss marriage. This was not to be, however, and although portrayed here in placid enough mood, Munch also made Tulla the model for Hate and The Murderess.

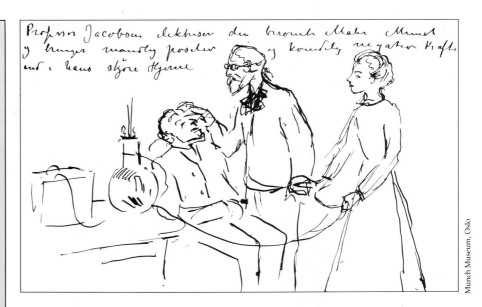

Munch Museum, Oslo

tuberculosis and mental illness convinced him it was unwise to marry, but he also feared marriage would interfere with his work. His first affair, with the headstrong wife of a medical officer, haunted him for years, while, in Berlin, he was attracted by Przybyszewski's wife, Dagny, and portrayed her as a temptress in *Jealousy*. His final, disastrous liaison with Tulla Larsen ended with her shooting off the joint of one of his fingers.

Although based in Germany, Munch travelled frequently, living in a succession of boarding houses. He was not a healthy man and his nomadic lifestyle must have mentally and physically exhausted him. Money was also a problem and, on one occasion, a patron rescued Munch after he had been evicted from his room and was forced to wander the streets of Berlin for three days without food.

Nevertheless, these were productive years. On a visit to Paris Munch met Paul Gauguin and his followers and, at Bing's Art Nouveau gallery, he saw the influential exhibition of Japanese woodcuts. Also in Paris, he developed his interest in new printing techniques, under the supervision of the renowned graphic artist, Auguste Clot.

IMPORTANT COMMISSIONS

Munch's major commissions at the turn of the century came from his friend, Dr Linde. In addition to a superb portrait of the doctor's four sons, the artist completed a folio of prints for him and drew up plans for a frieze to decorate his nursery. The latter was never executed, however, as Linde eventually decided that Munch's work might not be suitable for his children's room.

In 1906-7, he gained several other important commissions from Max Reinhardt, to provide a frieze for his new Kammerspiele theatre and design sets for Ibsen's *Ghosts* and *Hedda Gabler*. While he was working on these pictures, Munch lived in the theatre, painting by day and drinking by night. He kept himself remote from other

Self-parody
(above) Feelings of persecution brought about by the Larsen affair and criticism of his work led Munch to a breakdown in 1908. Here, the artist portrays himself receiving electric shock treatment.

people, causing a colleague to admit that 'He remained both a stranger and a puzzle to us'.

The shooting incident with Tulla Larsen, excessive drinking and exhaustion began to take their toll, and Munch became obsessed with feelings of persecution which were not helped by the abusive criticism of his work by his countrymen. Finally, in 1908, after a three-day drinking spree, he suffered a nervous breakdown and was admitted to Daniel Jacobson's clinic in Copenhagen. There, he recuperated for eight months, receiving various forms of therapy.

Munch had always been aware of the danger inherent in allowing his creativity to feed off his neuroses, but chose to ignore it. 'I would not cast off my illness' he had written 'for there is much in my art that I owe to it.' Now, however, he dedicated himself to recovery. In doing so, he made a conscious decision to abandon the obsessive, neurotic imagery of the past. Henceforward, he would depict the things he saw around him, rather than his emotions.

In addition, Munch resolved to put an end to his wandering. Hitherto, he had spent only his summers in Norway, at Åsgårdstrand, but now he returned there permanently, settling at first in the coastal town of Kragerø.

Ironically, the ending of Munch's most creative period coincided with greater official recognition. In 1908, he was made a Knight of the Order of St

The search for peace
(right) After his breakdown, Munch resolved to abandon the emotional images of his past and dedicate himself to mental recovery. He moved to Norway and produced much calmer works but he was still far from calm himself. He was an insomniac and would often book an overnight couchette to Oslo as he found sleeping on trains easier.

The artist and 'his family'
(below) Munch called his paintings 'his children' and littered his studio at Ekely with them. However, despite his fatherly proclamation, many were left in the open air regardless of the weather, while others were strewn across his studio floor.

H. Roger Viollet

Olav and, in 1911, he won the prestigious competition for decorating the University Assembly Hall. Here, he installed a new *Frieze of Life*, although this time he chose to portray universal forces – *The Sun, History, Alma Mater* – rather than the inner workings of the soul.

FINAL PROJECTS

Munch aimed to produce further public murals. In particular, he cherished the idea of designing a frieze on the theme of working men and industry. Preliminary sketches were displayed in the dining room of the Freia Chocolate Factory in 1922 but, sadly, the project never materialized. Munch also offered his services for the decoration of the new City Hall in Oslo, but the building work was delayed until 1933, by which time the artist had an eye complaint and could no longer paint.

Munch's last years were spent in isolation at his estate in Ekely. Here, he lived a spartan life, surrounded by the paintings which he called his 'children'. Despite this term of affection, he treated them badly, littering his prints on the floor and hanging his paintings out on the apple trees to dry.

With the rise of the Nazis, Munch's art was branded as degenerate and his pictures sold off from German museums. Then, in December 1943, he contracted a fatal dose of bronchitis after a bomb blew out the windows of his house. He died on 23 January 1944. In his will, he generously bequeathed his entire collection of prints and paintings – some 20,000 in all – to the city of Oslo.

Munch Museum, Oslo

Images of the Soul

Munch's belief that art should be of 'people who breathe, who feel emotions, who suffer and love' resulted in unprecedented images of the innermost feelings and mental anguish of modern man.

Rasmus Meyers Samlinger, Bergen

Jealousy (1895)
(left) One of the early paintings in the Frieze of Life, Jealousy *combines the themes of passion and jealousy with the biblical allegory of temptation. The isolated foreground figure has the features of the artist's Polish friend Stanislaw Przybyszewski, while the seductress in the background is portrayed as Eve, the temptress, picking the fateful apple.*

When Munch died, there was a copy of Dostoevsky's book *The Devils* by his bedside. It seems a fitting choice for a man who created his own nightmare visions and who provided the earliest pictorial definitions of paranoia and angst. Munch himself did little to dispel this image, claiming that art was his life's blood, costing him pain and suffering.

Initially, his personal style was built up from his own subjective view of the world around him. After his early naturalist phase, Munch's first important paintings – including *The Sick Child* (p.120) – were described as 'impressionistic' by the critics, at a time when the word was used as a term of abuse. But rather than studying the variations of light caused by the weather or the time of day, Munch chose to concentrate on the momentary visual distortions that can occur as the eye adjusts to different conditions – in effect, tricks of the light. As a result, most early commentators singled out Munch's apparently cavalier use of colour for their criticisms.

From this position, it was a short step to progress from painting visual impressions to depicting the effect that these impressions had on the emotions. *The Scream* (p.122) is the most famous example of this. Munch was inspired by a dramatic sunset which he had witnessed while walking beside a fjord. However, by suppressing his own features and by transforming the waters and the sky into threatening shock waves of vibrant colour, he managed to convey the feelings of terror that he had experienced on that occasion. Munch defended his approach by stressing that 'Nature is the means, not the end. If one can attain something by changing nature, one must do it.'

This directness was reflected in Munch's method of working. When, for example, he was commissioned to paint a portrait of the industrialist, Herbert Esche, Munch did nothing for the first fortnight except stay with the family until he felt he knew his subject. Then he set to work very rapidly, testing his colours on his client's expensive wallpaper and relying on a

simple charcoal sketch on the canvas as his sole guide for the composition.

During his Symbolist phase (c.1889-1900), Munch turned to the depiction of ideas rather than emotions, using the mystical and sexual images that were fashionable as the basis for his *Frieze of Life*. In fact, the very notion of a frieze, with its attempt to simulate the resonant quality of music, was a thoroughly Symbolist concept.

KEY IMAGES

For the several components of his *Frieze*, Munch selected a few key images and reworked them constantly, varying the colour schemes, the poses of the figures or even just the titles. 'Art is crystallization' he asserted, convinced that his revisions would eventually lead to the most powerfully emotive version of any given theme.

In this regard, Munch's interest in the graphic arts proved crucial. Originally, he had taken up etching, in 1894, as a means of earning extra income. However, as the possibilities of the medium became apparent to him, he grew more inventive and, at one stage, even acquired the habit of carrying a copper plate around in his pocket to use like a sketch book.

Bathing Men (1907-8)
(above) This painting forms the central panel in a triptych of bathers representing Youth, Manhood and Old Age, and shows man's harmony with nature. The light colouring and new subject matter reflect the artist's search for peace with life.

Girls on the Jetty (1899)
(left) Munch repeated this composition numerous times in various mediums. In it he evokes the quiet mood of a clear mid-summer night, using subtle shades which contrast with the brightly coloured figures on the jetty.

Dr Jacobson (1909)
(right) Munch painted portraits throughout his life, and although the full-length pose of Dr Jacobson is typical of other male portraits, the brilliant colouring is a unique product of Munch's disturbed state of mind at the time.

Munch's work in Paris, in 1896, with Auguste Clot – the printer who had aided Toulouse-Lautrec and Bonnard – proved a revelation. He learnt the techniques of making lithographs and colour woodcuts and, to the latter in particular, he brought exciting innovations. By sawing the woodblock into smaller sections and colouring these individually, he was able to produce multicoloured woodcuts easily, without going through the tedious process of making separate printings for each colour.

Prints were invaluable to Munch because the plates or blocks could easily be reworked or printed in different colours, thereby greatly increasing the scope for experiment. There was also a degree of feedback from the prints to his canvases: compositions were often refined in lithographs or woodcuts and then translated back into paint, producing a simplified and more powerful image.

In his later years, Munch grew increasingly reluctant to part with his paintings and, where he was obliged to sell, frequently made replicas for himself. In his heart, he still nurtured hopes of displaying his works together, confident that the full force of his very personal style could only be appreciated if viewed en masse.

The availability of his art to a wide public was of prime importance to Munch and, in a sense, this single desire governed his interest in friezes, graphic work and large murals. He despised the notion of a bourgeois art, where the academies became factories for producing paintings which vanished into the houses of the wealthy forever.

COMPARISONS

Working People

From the beginning of his career, Munch sketched and painted local people, including the agricultural workers on the farm where his family spent each summer, and from 1908 onwards workers became a central theme in his work. The subject had become popular in the 19th century. In France, there were political overtones, initially, in the paintings of Gustave Courbet, while Jean-François Millet and Vincent van Gogh preferred to treat their peasant subjects with compassion and grandeur. In England, the writings of John Ruskin and, later, William Morris, stressed the value of workmanship and gave rise to a number of picturesque depictions of labour by Pre-Raphaelite painters like Ford Madox Brown and William Bell Scott.

National Museum Vincent van Gogh, Amsterdam

A. C. Cooper/National Trust Photographic Library

William Bell Scott (1811-90) Iron and Coal *(left) Scottish painter and poet, William Bell Scott is best known for his series of eight paintings representing Northumberland history – a commission he won on the recommendation of Ruskin. Iron and Coal is the last and finest painting in the series and glorifies contemporary industrial life on Tyneside.*

Vincent van Gogh (1853-90) Peasant Woman Tying Sheaves *(above) One of the most influential artists of the 19th century, Van Gogh painted many agricultural workers during the last two years of his life, often basing his paintings on compositions by Millet. His early work as a lay preacher led him to invest his peasant subjects with true dignity.*

After Munch's return to Norway in 1908 his paintings lost their emotional intensity, and he turned to his native landscape, nature and working people for the subjects of his work. These themes were central to his large-scale public projects such as the University murals and the frieze at the Freia chocolate factory. But even in his apparently realistic works, traces of his old obsessions are still discernible. The bowed head of the model in his *Nude by the Wicker Chair* (right) carries faint echoes of the shy apprehension of the young girl in *Puberty* (p.121), while the workmen in *Workers Returning Home* (p.129) have the same remorseless frontality as the faceless figures in *Anxiety* (p.123).

Munch was, in every sense, an isolated figure. He had no pupils and he declined invitations to join avant-garde groups like *Die Brücke*. Even to his bohemian friends in Christiania and Berlin, he had remained something of an outsider. However, his haunting images linking the themes of sickness, death and raw, sexual power neatly encapsulated the mystical spirit of the Symbolists, while the directness of his style, with its daringly inventive distortions, paved the way for Expressionism.

Nude by the Wicker Chair (1929)

(right and detail below) Late works like this nude show Munch's sensitive handling of colour and his concern with the quality of his painting. The mood is created by the model's shy, downcast head, which seems to isolate her in the light, airy room, and the contrast between the cool colours which describe the contours of her body and the warm colours of the blanket and the background.

Munch Museum, Oslo

Barrie Thorpe

Lines of Colour

Munch's apparently bizarre use of colour was the result of a conscious desire to paint more than a straightforward rendering of the exterior world. Colours and patterns were, above all, a means of creating mood and, more importantly, of expressing man's inner emotion. In later works like the nude above, Munch's brushwork becomes more expressive and lines of colour are used to describe form itself.

THE MAKING OF A MASTERPIECE

The Dance of Life

Painted between 1899 and 1900, *The Dance of Life* belongs to the section of Munch's *Frieze of Life* called 'Dawning Love'. The composition evolved from *The Three Stages of Woman* – an earlier work which showed three aspects of womanhood in the figures of virgin, whore and nun. The same three figures appear here, where the central image of the passionate woman is a powerful symbol of sexual allure. The dance theme fittingly illustrates the cyclical nature of Munch's *Frieze*, while the 'curving shoreline and ever moving sea' were constant motifs, binding together the griefs and loves that link generation to generation.

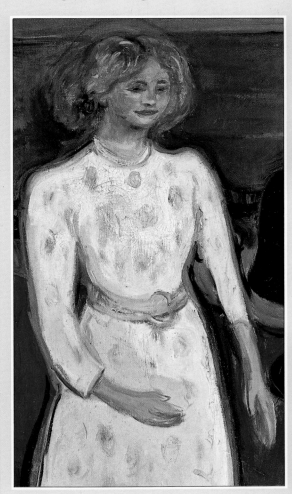

The innocent girl
(above) The white dress of the young girl on the left of the painting denotes her innocence. Possibly modelled on Munch's friend Tulla Larsen, she gazes expectantly at the centre figures, and appears to be stepping forward, as though eager to join in the dance of life and love.

'Just as Leonardo da Vinci studied human anatomy and dissected corpses, so I try to dissect souls.'
Edvard Munch

Attraction (1896)
(below) The central couple in The Dance of Life *were based on figures in this earlier lithograph. The woman's flowing hair – a frequent motif in Munch's work – envelops and ensnares the man.*

Munch Museum, Oslo

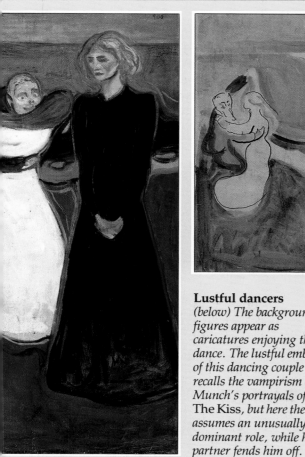

A preliminary sketch
(left) This lively sketch, dated 1898, shows that Munch's original idea was to show 'a young priest dancing with a woman with flowing hair' on a light summer's night. The other dancers became less animated in the final painting, where the figures of the women dominate the foreground. But the moon and its cylindrical reflection remain a powerful symbol of fertility and bathe the composition in a mystical golden light.

Munch Museum, Oslo

Lustful dancers
(below) The background figures appear as caricatures enjoying the dance. The lustful embrace of this dancing couple recalls the vampirism of Munch's portrayals of **The Kiss**, but here the man assumes an unusually dominant role, while his partner fends him off.

National Gallery, Oslo

The woman in black
(right) The figure on the right of the painting is usually interpreted as death or the nun (that is, the death of sexuality). An ageing woman, she stands alone, bitter and disillusioned, a spectator of a dance in which she has no hope of ever participating.

Gallery

Munch was one of the key artists in overthrowing the idea that painting is concerned fundamentally with imitating natural appearances. He depicted man's inner life with an intensity that at times approached frenzy, and his greatest works treat overpowering emotions such as fear and sex (these two often combined) with

The Sick Child *1885-86*
47" × 46¾" National Gallery, Oslo

This painting, of which Munch made several other versions, was inspired by his childhood experiences of sickness and death. Detail is reduced to a minimum, and the eye is immediately drawn to the figure of the child whose pale face contrasts with her red hair. We see both the yearning in the child's eyes and the mother's pain.

unprecedented psychological conviction and subtlety. The Scream is the most famous of all his works and the prime example of how he abandoned naturalism to gain emotional impact, and works such as Puberty and Anxiety show how poignantly and eloquently he portrayed the mental conflicts that beset mankind.

After he recovered from a nervous breakdown in 1908, Munch's work became much less introspective. He painted the working people of Norway with great vigour, his landscapes show a new love of Nature, and in his murals for Oslo University he proved himself one of the most glorious decorative artists of the 20th century.

Puberty *1893*
59″ × 43¾″ National Gallery, Oslo

The awakening of sexual feelings was one of Munch's recurring themes. Adolf Paul, a member of Munch's circle in Berlin, described the work in progress: 'On the edge of the bed a naked girl was sitting. She did not look like a saint, yet there was something innocent, coy and shy in her manner . . . these qualities prompted Munch to paint her.'

121

The Scream *1893*
36″ × 29″ National Gallery, Oslo

*'One evening', wrote Munch, 'I was walking along a path, the city
on one side, the fjord below. I felt tired and ill . . . The sun was
setting and the clouds turning blood-red. I sensed a scream passing
through Nature; it seemed to me that I heard the scream. I painted
this picture, painted the clouds as actual blood. The colour shrieked.'*

Anxiety *1894*
37" × 28¾" Munch Museum, Oslo

*In the 1902 Berlin Secession exhibition, Munch hung a series of his
paintings around four walls of the entrance hall to form his Frieze of
Life. Anxiety hung on the same wall as The Scream, a wall
representing 'Fear of Life'. 'There was a symphonic effect', wrote Munch,
'it made a great stir – a lot of antagonism – and a lot of approval.'*

The Dance of Life *1899-1900*
49½″ × 75″ National Gallery, Oslo

This is one of the pictures that made up Munch's Frieze of Life, *an ambitious series of works that never had a definitive form. 'The frieze is conceived', he wrote, 'as a series of paintings which together present a picture of life. Through the whole series runs the undulating line of the seashore. Beyond that line is the ever-moving sea, while beneath the trees is life in all its fullness, its variety, its joys and sufferings.' Here the dancing figures represent physical desire, but in the midst of passion there is loneliness, and the mournful figure on the right suggests the transitoriness of all feelings.*

The Sun *1909-11*
178″ × 310″ Oslo University

Munch's huge murals in the Great Hall of Oslo University were the greatest public commission of his career and he responded with work of inspired boldness. The murals represent the powerful forces of eternity, and here the sun is portrayed as the source of life, its rays illuminating the sea and the rocky landscape of the Kragerø fjord.

Winter in Kragerø *1912*
51¾″ × 51½″ Munch Museum, Oslo

*When he returned to Norway in 1909, after living mainly in
Germany since 1892, Munch spent much of his time at Kragerø and
he painted some splendid pictures of its rough coastal scenery. This is
perhaps the most monumental of them, the vigorous composition
dominated by the magnificent form of the pine tree.*

Workers Returning Home *1915*
79½″ × 90½″ Munch Museum, Oslo

This is generally regarded as the most commanding of the series of pictures of workers that Munch painted around this time. Although he was not a politically militant artist, he identified strongly with the working class. He must have been familiar with such scenes since his youth in Grünerløkka, when he lived near a large sailcloth factory.

The Lonely Ones *c.1935*
39″ × 51″ Munch Museum,
Oslo

*Munch often reworked his
compositions over a long period
and he had painted a similar
picture 40 years earlier,
although here the colours have a
new electrifying quality. Figures
standing on the seashore were
one of his favourite themes,
suggesting the insignificance
and insecurity of man against
the magnitude of Nature, and
often conveying a sense of
isolation and melancholy.*

Munch's Berlin

Norway's puritanical climate encouraged native artists and writers to travel abroad. In the 1890s, Munch settled in Berlin and became part of an avant-garde group which changed the course of European art.

The first exhibition of Munch's work in Berlin opened on 5 November 1892, and closed just one week later amid a storm of protest and criticism from the press. Yet as Munch later remarked, 'I could not have asked for better publicity. I never had so much fun'.

Certainly, the furious reaction to what one conservative newspaper described as 'Munch's smearings' was entirely predictable. Berlin in the last decade of the 19th century was a city of staunchly conservative tastes. The wealthy middle classes spent their mornings in the café discussing the latest fashions from Paris, their afternoons taking tea in the salon, and their evenings at the Opera. When the Kaiser rode at the head of his

Prussian troops, respectable people thronged the streets to cheer these symbols of German military might and imperialist ambition.

But behind the opulent palaces and expensive restaurants lay the seamier side of Berlin: the decaying, rat-infested slums of the working class quarter, the teeming beer halls and the brothels of the red-light districts. And it was in the twilight zone between these two worlds, between the splendour of the Avenue Unter den Linden and the squalor of the back streets, that Berlin's bohemia thrived.

A small tavern called the Black Piglet served as the main meeting place of Berlin's alternative set – a floating population of Scandinavians, Jewish

The Café Bauer
(below) An altogether more elegant meeting place than the cramped rooms of the Black Piglet, the Café Bauer was another of Munch's favourite haunts. Situated on the fashionable Avenue Unter den Linden, the Café Bauer was commonly used by members of the city's bohemia as their Berlin postal address.

H. Roger Viollet

A dramatist of disquiet
(above) One of the founders of modern theatre, August Strindberg came from Sweden to live in Berlin in 1892. He found many friends including Munch, who shared Strindberg's belief that art should express the disorder of the human soul.

Archiv für Kunst und Geschichte

intellectuals and German artists in rebellion against the Prussian spirit. It was here that the obscure young men, who were later to change the direction of European art, met to drink, discuss and quarrel about their work, their careers and about the times in which they lived.

Only August Strindberg, the 'father' of the group, had achieved fame by the time Munch arrived in Berlin. A restless and frequently aggressive genius, Strindberg had fled his Sweden in 1892, dogged by debts, a traumatic divorce from his first wife Siri von Essen, and a prosecution for blasphemy arising out of his short story *Getting Married*. He would often behave abysmally towards the younger artists. Munch tells how Strindberg used to trip him up and leave him lying on the pavement, much to the amusement of his friends and passers-by. Only when Munch threatened to give the older man a beating, did Strindberg cease this particular prank.

A WILD MYSTIC

Perhaps because of Strindberg's overbearing personality, Munch was more naturally drawn towards the young Polish writer Stanislaw Przybyszewski. Known to his friends as 'Stachu', Przybyszewski was the spiritual leader of the young artists. Like Strindberg, Stachu was obsessed by sexuality and mysticism. One night, the vision of hell which the Norwegian sculptor Gustav Vigeland conjured up to his friends was so intense that Stachu took flight. He was eventually

Munch Museum, Oslo

found in the woodshed, squatting naked on a pile of logs, convinced that he was Satan.

Certainly, Stachu dabbled in black magic and was fascinated by the occult, so much so that he never fulfilled the promise of his early years. But he was a brilliant interpreter of Chopin's music. Munch described him as 'nervous and moody, sometimes up in the skies, sometimes on the brink of despair'. In the tavern, Stachu would suddenly leap to his feet and rush to the piano. In the silence

The bohemian critic
(*left*) *The avant-garde writer and critic, 'Stachu', was one of the leaders of the circle who met in the Black Piglet. In 1894, a year before Munch painted this portrait, Stachu co-wrote the first defence of Munch's art.*

Mythical macabre
Akseli Gallen-Kallela was the most important of the Scandinavian artists associated with Munch during his Berlin period. Like Munch, Gallen-Kallela grew to reject naturalism as inadequate, although his own inspiration was found in Finnish myth. In this macabre painting, he depicts a scene from the epic poem, The Kalevala. *One of the heroes of the poem has been drowned in a river and his mother, using her black arts, attempts to rebuild the lifeless body.*

Akseli Gallen-Kallela/Lemmingkäinen's Mother/Art Museum of the Ateneum, Helsinki

The beautiful Ducha
(left) Dagny Juell –
nicknamed 'Ducha' – was
a 25-year-old art student
when she joined Munch's
circle. Renowned for her
seductive beauty, she had
tempestuous affairs with
Strindberg and other
members of the group,
before marrying Stachu.
With her flowing red hair,
she appears as the model
in many of Munch's most
famous paintings.

that followed the first chord, Chopin's beautiful music would flow through the room, so that the listeners became 'transfixed, spellbound, oblivious of time and place until the final echoes died away.'

However, Stachu also held another attraction for Munch – his wife Dagny Juell. Slim, beautiful and sensual, Ducha, as she was known by the young artists, was herself a writer of great talent. It was she who gave the name *Pan* to the magazine Stachu edited, which served as the defiant manifesto of the radical young artists in Berlin. The art historian Julius Meier-Graefe recalled how the group would gather in Przybyszewski's dimly lit room in Luisenstrasse: 'Against the wall by the door stood an upright piano, a peculiar instrument. It could be toned down by means of a lever, so that the other inmates of the house were not disturbed even when Stachu hammered on it with his fists. One of us would dance with Ducha, while the others looked on from the table: one spectator was Munch, the other was generally Strindberg. The four men in the room were all in love with Ducha, but they never showed it.' Whether Munch was really in love with Ducha is doubtful, for he shrank from close relationships with women. Certainly though, he was fascinated by Ducha's mysterious sexuality, and the themes of jealousy, anxiety and despair recur in his Berlin paintings.

A BOHEMIAN ESCAPE

At other times, the group would gather in Pakow at the villa of the lyric poet Richard Dehmel, whose temperament was so violent and unpredictable

that even Strindberg described him as 'a wild man'. In Pakow, the artists could escape the grime of the city and enjoy excursions into the surrounding countryside. But the evenings were dedicated to art. Dehmel with his dark and brooding features, would begin by reciting his latest poem. Then Stachu would play Chopin or Schumann on Dehmel's grand piano, accompanied by the Norwegian poet Sigbjorn Obstfelder on violin. Obstfelder would also recite

The new artists
(above) In revolt against the traditional art establishment, the Berliner Secession *was a breakaway group of artists formed in 1898. This poster advertises their first exhibition, held the following year.*

his poems in the original Norwegian, relying upon the striking rhythm and sound to convey the meaning of his work.

However, these cultural evenings could also degenerate into drinking sessions which lasted well into the next day. As ever, the beautiful Dachu was the centre of attraction for the young men, although she alone seemed oblivious to the effects of the alcohol which they all drank so liberally. Tragically, Ducha was later killed by a jealous young Russian in Tiblis, who shot her through the head with a revolver before killing himself.

THE NEW ARTISTS

As Munch himself had suggested, it was the storm of publicity that accompanied his exhibition at the Berlin Artists Club in 1892 that launched his career. After the Club approved a motion by the painter Anton von Werner to close down the exhibition, a number of progressive artists, led by Max Liebermann and Ludwig von Hofmann, formed the *Gruppe XI* which became the Berlin Secession, founded in 1898. The next year, the Secession held its own exhibition, although Munch was still considered far too outrageous to be invited to take part.

It was not until 1902 that pictures from Munch's *Frieze of Life* were displayed at the Secessionist exhibition. The exhibition marked a turning point in Munch's career. But more importantly, it represented a turning point in the artistic climate of Berlin itself. The young artists who met at the Black Piglet had set in motion a new era of radical innovation, especially in painting and literature. With the turn of the century another generation of artists took up the banner of rebellion against traditional German values.

Zoë Dominic

Munch himself returned to Berlin in 1906 and 1907 to paint a new Frieze for the foyer of Max Reinhardt's theatre, The Kammerspiele. He also designed sets for Reinhardt's production of Ibsen's *Ghosts* and *Hedda Gabler*. But by then, the Black Piglet was part of a by-gone era. Indeed the centre of German art was shifting towards Dresden and Munich. Not until the heady years of the 1920s did Berlin actually recapture the title of Germany's Bohemia.

Hedda Gabler
(above) Munch was to return to Berlin in 1906 to design the sets and costumes for a production of Hedda Gabler – *a play written by the inspired Norwegian dramatist, Henrik Ibsen. Munch developed a fascination for the central character, Hedda, who shoots herself in the final act of the play. The British actress, Janet Suzman, is shown here in the role.*

Meeting on the Beach/Munch Museum, Oslo

The Reinhardt frieze
(left) Ibsen's producer in Berlin was Max Reinhardt, whose theatre – the Kammerspiele – was the most innovative in Europe. Munch and Reinhardt became close friends, and in 1907 Munch agreed to paint this picture – one of his celebrated studies for the Frieze of Life – *to be displayed in the theatre's foyer.*

135

A Year in the Life 1905

In 1905, Munch's native Norway won independence from Sweden. In the same year Russia suffered catastrophic defeats at the hands of Japan and was plunged into a revolutionary ferment. Meanwhile German blustering over French interests in North Africa provoked the first Moroccan crisis.

Although Norway and Sweden had been united by the same monarch since 1814, the former still retained its own parliament (the Storting) to govern internal affairs. A growing national consciousness echoed by an explosive literary revival at the end of the 19th century led to the Storting's demand for Norwegian political autonomy. An act was passed setting up a separate consular service which was repudiated by King Oscar II. In June 1905, the Storting declared 'the union with Sweden dissolved as a result of the King ceasing to function as Norwegian King', confirmed by a plebiscite in August. War seemed imminent for a time, but in October a formal separation was negotiated. In December, Prince Charles of Denmark became Norway's new King as Haakon VII.

Russia had been at war with Japan over the control of

Arrogant Kaiser
(left) In 1905 a united German Empire had only been in existence for 34 years. Bismarck, its creator, had been ousted by the new Kaiser, Wilhelm II, in 1890, from which time German foreign policy took an increasingly dangerous turn. The Kaiser, who was set on making Germany a top-league power, was unstable and lacked the wide vision, subtlety and concentration essential in a great leader. The Morocco Crisis of 1905-6 was sparked off by his attempt to test the new Anglo-French entente over colonial possessions by offering German backing to the Sultan (Morocco was under French mandate). During his Mediterranean cruise in March, Wilhelm II paid an ostentatious visit to Tangier, later calling for an international conference. But the Kaiser's triumph was to be shortlived.

E. T. Archive

'Bloody Sunday'
(right) The discontent of the Russian people with low wages, bad conditions, heavy taxation and lack of civil rights led to mass strikes and outright revolt against the Tsarist régime. On Sunday, 22 January, 150,000 people peacefully marched towards the Winter palace in St Petersburg. Led by Father George Gapon, organizer of the Union of Russian Factory Workers, their intention was to present a signed appeal to Tsar Nicholas II, whom they were sure was ignorant of their plight. Soldiers fired into the crowd when it refused to disperse and within minutes many hundred were dead and 3,000 wounded. On that day illusions of a beneficent monarchy were destroyed and Russia was on the road to Revolution.

Manchuria and Korea since 1904. On 1 January the naval base of Port Arthur (leased from China by the Russians) fell to the Japanese after a ten-month siege. Three months later the Russian army was defeated in a hard-fought battle at Mukden.

BATTLE OF TSUSHIMA

The final blow was struck in May when the Russian Baltic fleet arrived in the straits of Tsushima, between Korea and Japan, after a journey halfway round the world, only to be utterly destroyed by the Japanese Imperial Navy led by Admiral Togo. Both victor and vanquished were exhausted by the war and ready for peace. The terms of the Treaty of Portsmouth in September 1905 were relatively moderate. Russia gave up Port

Arthur and the southern half of Sakhalin Island and recognized Japan's predominant position in Korea. The two powers later agreed to exercise equal influence in Manchuria.

Defeat further discredited the already unpopular Tsarist regime. The ensuing '1905 Revolution' began on 22 January with 'Bloody Sunday', when a peaceful demonstration of 150,000 workers and their families was fired on outside the Winter Palace. About a thousand were killed and many more wounded. Strikes, demonstrations and peasant risings swept the land, culminating in October, when sailors of the battleship *Potemkin* mutinied and 200,000 urban workers organized their own representative body, the St Petersburg *soviet*, soon to be dominated by the fiery personality of 25-year-old Leon Trotsky. The new prime minister, Sergei Witte, persuaded the Tsar that

Japanese propaganda
(right) This comic map of Europe was issued by the Japanese in 1904 to vilify Russian territorial ambitions. Japan was also seeking an empire on the Chinese mainland and had already quarrelled with Russia over Port Arthur and Korea in the decade before war was declared in 1904. Within a year, Russian overconfidence had been humbled.

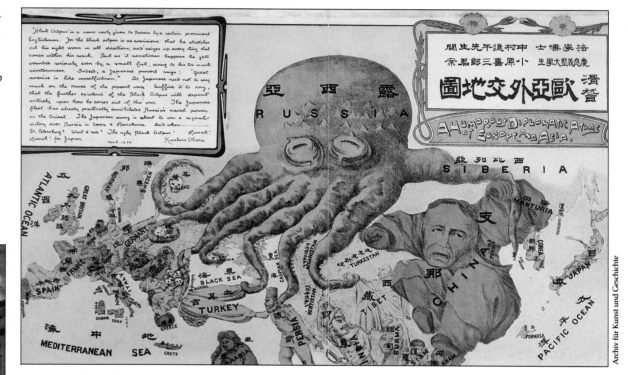

Archiv für Kunst und Geschichte

Russian prisoner at Port Arthur
(right) The Russo-Japanese war began in February 1904. The main war zone was the Russian-controlled Port Arthur, an ice-free harbour on the southern tip of the Liaotung peninsula in Manchuria. Japanese successes in blockading and partially destroying the Russian fleet encouraged the landing of troops in June under General Nogi. However, progress south to Port Arthur was delayed by the Russians who were busy fortifying the town. Three months of Japanese assaults proved suicidal so Nogi decided to launch a triple attack on the twin peaks of 203 Metre Hill in November which was gained after 10 days, at a loss of 8,000 men. From this vantage Japanese heavy guns bombarded the Russian fleet and town into submission. The Russian General Stoessel officially surrendered on 2 January 1905.

Novosti

Johnson Archive

the token consultative body (Duma) he had set up was insufficient and wider promises of reform were made.

The careful balance of European power threatened to be undermined during this year by Kaiser Wilhelm II's blustering attempts at world power status. His personal visit to Tangier was an attempt to block the Anglo-French *entente cordiale* whereby France recognized Britain's position in Egypt while Britain acknowledged French interests in Morocco. The Kaiser's tacit recognition of Moroccan independence only succeeded in strengthening the Anglo-French alliance. Another blow fell when the treaty agreed between Kaiser Wilhelm and the Tsar at Björkö in Finland later that year was repudiated by ministers on both sides as it conflicted with the terms of the existing Franco-Russian alliance.

A variety of other events characterized 1905. It was the year the great actor-manager Sir Henry Irving, whose knighthood set the seal of respectability on the theatre, died and the Swedish film star Greta Garbo was born. The artists Schmidt-Rottluff and Kirchner founded the expressionist *Die Brücke* (The Bridge) Group. The British General Election was a landslide victory for the Liberals, who were to remain in power, introducing a wide range of reforms, up to the First World War. In Dublin, a new militant organization, Sinn Fein, held its first national convention. Franz Lehar's operetta *The Merry Widow* began its world-wide triumph at Vienna while Richard Strauss's more decadently erotic *Salome* received its first performance at Dresden; and, not to be outdone, Dr Sigmund Freud published his *Three Essays on the Theory of Sexuality*.

An immediate sensation

(right) Claude Debussy wrote that his 'music has no other aim than to melt in the minds of predisposed people and to become identified with certain scenes or objects'. The composer was very much alive to the literary and artistic currents of his time, particularly Symbolism and Impressionism. In 1894, he completed a musical equivalent to Mallarmé's celebrated Symbolist poem Prélude à l'après-midi d'une faune, *a revolutionary piece of music which was followed 11 years later by his great Impressionist work* La mer. *This striking musical evocation of the sea found pictorial inspiration in the seascapes of Turner and the prints of the Japanese artists Hokusai and Hiroshige; hence the use of the Hokusai print on the first edition of the work.*

CLAUDE DEBUSSY

LA MER

British Library

Archiv für Kunst und Geschichte

Genius of modern physics

(left) In 1905, Albert Einstein (1879-1955) published three important papers containing revolutionary theories: that light is a combination of energy and frequency; that the irregular motion of particles in liquid suspension (Brownian Motion) was due to kinetic energy, and finally his special theory of relativity which destroyed the Newtonian concept of absolute time and space and asserted that their measurement was dependent on relative motion. Furthermore, energy (E) was linked with mass (M) and the speed of light (C) in the equation $E=MC^2$.

GALLERY GUIDE

Rossetti

The majority of Rossetti's works are still in Britain. The Tate Gallery, London, owns the largest single collection, including early PRB works and a selection from his gallery of beautiful women. The latter are also in evidence at Manchester (City Art Gallery) and at Birmingham (City Museum and Barber Institute), while both the Victoria and Albert Museum, London, and the Fitzwilliam Museum, Cambridge, have impressive collections of the artist's graphic work. Important paintings can also be seen, in situ, at the Oxford Union at the University and at Llandaff Cathedral, Cardiff. In the United States, Rossetti's most famous picture is the unfinished *Found* (Delaware Art Museum, Wilmington) and the same gallery also contains the stunning *Veronica Veronese*. The Fogg Museum of Art, Harvard, possesses a version of *The Blessed Damozel*, and the University Museum, Lawrence, Kansas owns a depiction of Jane Morris.

Redon

Redon's reputation was forged with his marvellous series of lithographs, of which the most comprehensive collection is in the Bibliothèque Nationale, Paris. In a similar vein are his charcoal drawings and the most extensive displays of these are at the Kröller-Müller State Museum, Otterlo and at the Musée des Beaux-Arts, Bordeaux. Best-represented in American collections are his brilliantly coloured pastels, most notably at Chicago, Cleveland and New York. Redon's oils are less common and the most celebrated examples are in the Musée d'Orsay, Paris, and in the Metropolitan Museum of Art, New York (the remarkable *Pandora*).

Munch

At his death, Munch left his vast personal collection – consisting of 1,000 paintings, 15,400 prints and 4,500 watercolours – to the city of Oslo. Accordingly, his most important works are now, almost exclusively, in either the Munch Museum or in the National Gallery, Oslo, while the City University contains his principal surviving mural commission. Bergen (Rasmus Meyers Samlinger) and Trondheim also own examples of his work. Elsewhere in Europe, there are major paintings in Sweden (Stockholm and Gothenburg), northern Germany (Lübeck and Bremen) and Switzerland (Zürich). In America, the best-known pictures by Munch are at the Museum of Fine Arts, Boston (*The Voice*) and the Museum of Modern Art, New York (*The Storm*).

Klimt

The greatest examples of Klimt's work are in his native city, Vienna. The Österreichische Galerie's collection encompasses all aspects of his career, and includes major projects such as the *Beethoven Frieze* and many of his most memorable Symbolist subjects. Also in Vienna, there are paintings at the Historisches Museum der Stadt (*Pallas Athene* and *Emilie Flöge*), while examples of Klimt's decorative work can be seen at the Kunsthistorisches Museum and the Burgtheater. Elsewhere, the most overtly Symbolist pictures are in Munich, Venice and Rome. There is little in this vein to be found in the United States, but examples of his portraits of women are housed in private collections in New York and Honolulu, while the Museum of Modern Art, New York, contains the curious landscape, *Park*.

BIBLIOGRAPHY

A. Comini, *Gustav Klimt*, Braziller, New York, 1975
B. & J. Dobbs, *Dante Gabriel Rossetti: An Alien Victorian*, Humanities, Atlantic Heights, 1977
Exhibition Catalogue, *Gustav Klimt and Egon Schiele*, Guggenheim Museum, New York, 1965
M. & D. Gerhardus, *Symbolism and Art Nouveau*, Phaidon, Oxford, 1979
R. Goldwater, *Symbolism*, Harper and Row, New York, 1979
J. P. Hodin, *Edward Munch*, Thames and Hudson, New York, 1985
P. Jullian (intro), *French Symbolist Painters*, Arts Council Exhibition, London, 1972
C. Keay, *Odilon Redon*, Academy Editions, London, 1977
E. Lucie-Smith, *Symbolist Art*, Thames & Hudson, New York, 1985
J. Nicoll, *Rossetti*, Studio Vista, London, 1975
R. Rosenblum (intro), *Edvard Munch: Symbols and Images*, National Gallery of Art, Washington, 1978
R. Stang, *Edvard Munch: the Man and His Art*, Abbeyville Press, New York, 1979
C. Wood, *The Pre-Raphaelites*, Viking, New York, 1981

Aubrey Beardsley (1872-98)

English graphic artist, a leading exponent of Aestheticism. Beardsley was precociously talented and largely self-taught, although his work owed much to the encouragement of Burne-Jones and to the study of Japanese prints. During his tragically brief career, he produced a stunning range of black-and-white illustrations, the most celebrated being those for Oscar Wilde's *Salomé* and those in *The Yellow Book*, a notorious periodical. Beardsley's achievement was to blend the supremely decorative qualities of the Art Nouveau style with the perverse imagery of the Decadents, thereby creating a beguiling marriage of beauty and evil. He died of tuberculosis at the age of 26.

Arnold Böcklin (1827-1901)

Swiss Symbolist painter, a forerunner of the Surrealists. Born in Basel and trained in Düsseldorf, Böcklin began as a landscapist but, after an extended stay in Rome (1850-57), he turned to classical subjects, evolving a personalized mythology that was dominated by brutal satyrs and sinister mermaids or nymphs. Increasingly, these figures participated in mood paintings, which did not illustrate specific events but took on the qualities of dreams. The most famous example is *The Island of the Dead* (for example, Metropolitan Museum, New York – Böcklin painted five versions), which combined a haunting blend of funereal motifs.

Sir Edward Coley Burne-Jones (1833-98)

English painter, a leading member of the second generation of Pre-Raphaelite artists. Burne-Jones studied at Oxford University, where he met William Morris and assisted Rossetti on the Union murals (1857). The latter gave him some informal tuition, but Burne-Jones's mature style owed more to his travels in Italy in 1859 and 1862. Through his studies of Renaissance art, he evolved his distinctive vision, which was epitomized by sequences of pale, androgynous women, inhabiting a dream-like, pseudo-classical world. Burne-Jones's works in this vein were enormously influential. Their exhibition at the Grosvenor Gallery (1877) placed him in the vanguard of the Aesthetic movement, while his inclusion in the Exposition Universelle of 1889 made him the hero of the French Symbolists. In addition to his paintings, Burne-Jones produced designs for tapestries, tiles and stained-glass windows (p.35).

James Ensor (1860-1949)

Belgian painter and graphic artist, whose work combines elements of Symbolism and Expressionism. Ensor's early paintings were Intimist in style and compare favourably with those of Bonnard and Vuillard. In 1884, he was a founder-member of *Les Vingt* and, through them, became acquainted with the latest Symbolist trends. However, his fiercely satirical masterpiece, *The Entry of Christ into Brussels* (1888, Musée Royal des Beaux-Arts, Antwerp) was too outrageous, even for that avant-garde body, and Ensor retreated into a self-martyring isolation. He chose to take refuge in his mother's shop in Ostend, which specialized in carnival masks and novelties, and he breathed life into this strange environment by portraying animated versions of these masks and costumes as the emblems of his persecution. Ensor's work anticipated many features of the Expressionist and Surrealist movements and his style had strong affinities with that of Munch.

Akseli Gallen-Kallela (1865-1931)

Finnish painter, dedicated to the creation of a national art. His early paintings were naturalistic but, after his arrival in Paris in 1884, Gallen-Kallela gradually assimilated the new Symbolist theories, finding them an ideal vehicle for his depiction of scenes from the Kalevala (p.133), the Finnish national epic. During the height of this Symbolist phase, he exhibited with Munch in Berlin (1895). In addition to painting, Gallen-Kallela was a versatile decorative artist; he produced designs for furniture and textiles, executed innovatory woodcuts and worked on large-scale frescoes, most notably those for the Finnish display at the World Fair of 1900.

Ferdinand Hodler (1853-1918)

Swiss artist associated with both the Symbolist and Jugendstil movements. Hodler studied in Geneva and completed his education with travels in France and Spain. His early style was naturalistic but, during his Symbolist period, he adopted a flat, linear approach that was strongly reminiscent of Puvis de Chavannes. The latter admired Hodler's work at the Exposition Universelle of 1889 and it was probably his success here that earned him the invitation to exhibit at the first Rosicrucian Salon in 1892. His most celebrated work is *Night* (1890, Kunstmuseum, Berne).

Fernand Khnopff (1858-1921)

Major Symbolist artist, a founder-member of *Les Vingt*. Khnopff was born in Belgium and trained there under Xavier Mellery, before completing his studies in Paris, where he admired the work of Delacroix and Moreau. However, Khnopff was a dedicated anglophile and the principal influence on his work came from the Pre-Raphaelites. In particular, Burne-Jones's androgynous women provided the prototype for his own, distinctive female type, although the Belgian invested them with an air of cruelty, thereby creating some of the most memorable images of the femme fatale.

Sir John Everett Millais (1829-96)
English painter, a founding member of the Pre-Raphaelite Brotherhood. Millais was a child prodigy and, at the age of eleven, became the youngest ever student at the Royal Academy Schools. There, he met Holman Hunt and, together with Rossetti, they formed the Pre-Raphaelite Brotherhood in 1848. Millais' strong colours and his ability to paint in meticulous detail made him particularly well-suited to the English strain of Symbolism. Between 1848 and 1857, he produced a lyrical series of elegiac paintings, of which *Autumn Leaves* is perhaps the most famous. With the recognition of his talents, however, Millais returned to more conventional artistic territory and much of his later career was devoted to portrait commissions and pictures of children. These, although technically superb, showed a decline in the inspirational qualities of his early work. In the year of his death he was honoured with the Presidency of the Royal Academy.

Gustave Moreau (1826-98)
Pioneering French painter; the linking figure between the Romantic and Symbolist movements. Moreau studied under Picot but was more influenced by Chassériau, sharing with him an admiration for the rich, colouristic style of Delacroix. He spent three years in Italy at the end of the 1850s and, on his return, concentrated on mythological subjects. His reputation was made, in 1864, by the appearance of *Oedipus and the Sphinx* at the Salon and the theme of the *femme fatale* was to dominate much of his subsequent painting, culminating in many trance-like visions of Salomé with the head of John the Baptist. Moreau was a solitary figure, shunning publicity and reluctant to sell his pictures. However, he was a most sympathetic teacher and his pupils at the Ecole des Beaux-Arts included Rouault and Matisse. Moreau's reputation declined after his death, until he was rediscovered by the Surrealists in the 1920s.

Pierre Puvis de Chavannes (1824-98)
French painter and decorative artist. Puvis was born in Lyons and studied in Paris, under Scheffer, Delacroix and Couture. He made his name with large-scale decorative works, the finest of which are at the Panthéon, in Paris. However, with the rise of Symbolism, Puvis' smaller canvases gained him a new and unexpected following. His most famous painting, *The Poor Fisherman* (pp.70-71), was much admired by Gauguin and Seurat, while *The Beheading of St John the Baptist* (1869, Barber Institute, Birmingham) was a seminal example of one of the most popular Symbolist subjects.

Félicien Rops (1833-98)
Belgian painter and graphic artist, active mainly in Paris. Rops began work as an illustrator, contributing lithographs to the satirical magazine *Uylenspiegel*. He arrived in Paris in 1862 and was rapidly drawn into the literary circles of the Symbolists. Admired by writers as diverse as Baudelaire, the Goncourt brothers and Huysmans, Rops forged his reputation with a series of startling engravings, most notably those for d'Aurevilly's *Les Diaboliques* and Péladan's *Le Vice Suprême*. In these, he brought the Decadent movement to the fringes of pornography, introducing elements of fetishism, cruelty and satanism. The macabre features of his work proved an influence on the young James Ensor.

Franz von Stuck (1863-1928)
Leading German Jugendstil artist. Stuck trained in Munich, where he became a co-founder of the Sezession in 1892. His early style was heavily influenced by Böcklin and this was combined with the prevailing imagery of the Decadents. *Femmes fatales* – usually in the guise of sphinxes or sirens – abounded in his work and his favourite subject, painted in more than a dozen versions after 1890, consisted of a nude woman surrendering to the embraces of a snake. Stuck's contribution to Jugenstil was highlighted by the villa which he designed for himself – a forerunner of Klimt's decorations at the Stoclet palace – and he was also important as a teacher. His pupils at the Munich Academy included Kandinsky, Albers and Klee.

Manoukian Collection, Paris

Who Shall Deliver Me?
With her enigmatic smile and hypnotic gaze, Khnopff's subject is the typical femme fatale.

INDEX